Fabrizio Mancinelli

CATACOMBS AND BASILICAS
The Early Christians in Rome

with an Introduction by
Umberto M. Fasola

This book is dedicated to the late Professor Enrico Josi, teacher of
generations of students of Christian archaeology, and for many years
Inspector of the Catacombs and Rector of the *Pontificio Istituto di
Archeologia Cristiana*. He has left us manifest evidence of his
versatility and his doctrine in the reorganization of the Pio Christian
Museum, of which he was the fervent director until the end of his
long and generous life.

In collaboration with the Pontificia Commissione di Archeologia Sacra
and the Vatican Museums (Pontifical Monuments, Galleries and Museums)

Scala, Firenze

1

Cover: Bust of Christ. Catacomb of Commodilla.

Frontispiece: Fresco in the crypt of Lucina in the catacomb of St. Callixtus. The basket of bread and the painted fish on the green field refer to the Miracle of the Loaves and Fishes, but the glass of red wine in the basket symbolizes the Eucharistic meal prefigured on that occasion.

Back-cover: Gilded glass with St. Agnes and a pair of doves. Catacomb of Pamphilus.

1 Painting in the Palazzo Apostolico Vaticano. It shows Piux IX's visit to the catacomb of St. Callixtus in 1854, after the discovery of the Crypt of the Popes and the tomb of St. Cecilia, shown here. The three saints portrayed in the skylight are the martyrs, Sebastian, Polycamus and Quirinus, who lie in the nearby catacomb of St. Sebastian. The next to last person on the right is Giovan Battista De Rossi, the great explorer and master scientist of Christian archaeology.

Contents

**
© COPYRIGHT 1981 by SCALA, Istituto Fotografico Editoriale, Firenze
Editorial Director: Francesco Papafava
Editing: Daniele Casalino
Editorial Assistant: Carlo Ghislandi
Layout: Fried Rosenstock
Translation: Carol Wasserman
Produced by SCALA, Istituto Fotografico Editoriale
Plans: SCALA
Photographs: SCALA (Mauro Sarri), except: n. 6, 7, 18 Biblioteca Apostolica Vaticana; n 2, 15 19, 26, 41, 48, 59, 81, 88 M. Carrieri; n. 84 A. Held; n. 36b, 37 F. Mancinelli; n. 1 Musei Vaticani; n. 24 T. Nicolini; n. 57, 62, 64, 85 Pontificia Commissione di Archeologia Sacra; n. 107 Publiaerfoto; n. 23 Reverenda Fabbrica di S. Pietro.
Printed in Italy by Conti Tipocolor Firenze 1981

ISBN 0-935748-13-X U.S. Pbk

2

Introduction

The illustrations for this book were collected by the late Professor Enrico Josi towards the end of a long and active life. The dissemination of knowledge about ancient Christian monuments — popularization in the higher sense of the term — formed an essential part of the professor's work, for he believed in the importance of these monuments as "venerable and authentic evidence of the faith and religious life of antiquity, and primary source material for the study of Christian institutions and culture'', to use the words of Pope Pius XI. He wrote articles, clear, comprehensible and brimming with details, for the *Osservatore Romano* and other newspapers, and dedicated the last years of his life to reorganizing the collections of the Museo Cristiano e Profano Lateranense (the Lateran

Museum) in their new lodgings in the Vatican. It was the ordinary visitor rather than the specialist that Professor Josi had in mind when he arranged the material for display in the new light-filled halls of the Vatican.

Thus, the sarcophagi and other sculptures were exhibited according to their subject matter, many casts were included of works exhibited elsewhere, and the great accomplishment of Giovan Battista De Rossi during the last century — the organization of the vast epigraphical collection along pedogogical lines — was left intact. As a result, an attentive visitor can easily grasp the essential aspects of the art, organization, beliefs and mentality of the Christians of the first centuries AD.

This book has the same popularizing aim. In its preparation Professor Josi deliberately brought together all the most characteristic pictures of the catacombs and other cult buildings, in order to provide a visual rather

2 Clivo di Scauro, with the Romanesque apse of Saints John and Paul, which was built on the remains of older Roman structures. The third-century façade of the church fronts on a steep hillside street. A Christian center in several of the building's rooms later became the "titulus" Byzantis or Bizans.

than a written synthesis of what modern archaeology has to say about the surviving traces of the early Christian Church in Rome. He wanted to create a real pictorial history of this early community, for of all the cities in the early Christian world it was probably Rome that left the largest number of historic remains in its cemeteries and churches and, above all, in the catacombs. Alas, that underground realm of death seems no longer to arouse the interest of a wide audience, now that scholars have robbed it of its former source of fascination, its supposed role as

3

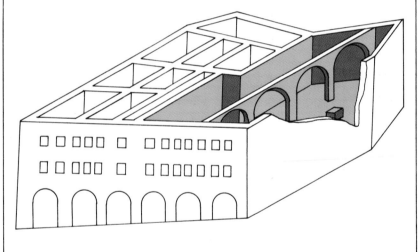

4

5

3 Row of "tabernae". A road through the Trajan marketplace gives an idea of the intense city life that went on in and around these shops. The Christians were undoubtedly a part of it.

4 Hypothetical reconstruction of the "domus ecclesia" beneath the basilica of Saints John and Paul. It was a two-story dwelling in whose right wing — marked in red — a large hall was built for the cult during the fourth century (from Frankl).

5 Praying figure. This was of the fourth century fresco decoration of the ground floor of the "domus ecclesia".

asylum and house of prayer for persecuted Christians. But science, today, can offer us instead images of a community of the faithful, with their daily ups and downs, the great events of their history, their worries and hopes and, above all, their religious sentiments, which are at least as fascinating in their own way. This community was an ancient one, directly connected with the first years of Christian preaching, and when St. Paul reached Rome in about AD 61 he found it already well-organized and efficient. The Christians had been informed of his arrival beforehand: immediately, they arranged for groups of representatives to welcome him with the honor and exultation befitting the great apostle, although he came in chains with other prisoners — perhaps common criminals — and an escort of soldiers. Groups of Christians hastened to the station on the Appian Way called Tres Tabernae, fifty kilometres from the city, and some went even farther, to the Forum Apii. The book of The Acts of the Apostles (28, 14-15) says that St. Paul was moved and drew courage from this fact, and was persuaded thereby that the Christian message had already grown deep roots in Rome. And indeed, these roots continued to grow and gain strength. In vain did Nero's persecution eliminate a "vast multitude" of believers (to use the expression of the pagan, Tacitus); in vain did tempests and disturbances strike again and again during the next two centuries: they caused the community trouble and pain, but they never shook its solid foundations.

The constant growth of the community forced its leaders to adopt more rational forms of organization, a step in keeping with the Roman spirit especially during a period when all the civilized world was governed from the city, and the Church was soon subdivided into groups — perhaps on the model of the enormous Jewish colony that already existed in Rome. In fact, the early Roman Christians retained a memory of their Jewish origins for quite a long time. As late as the fifth century, the two traditions were represented in basilica mosaics (in Santa Pudenziana (109) and Santa Sabina, for example) by the symbolic figures of the ecclesia ex circumcisione and the ecclesia ex gentibus. It is almost certain that no

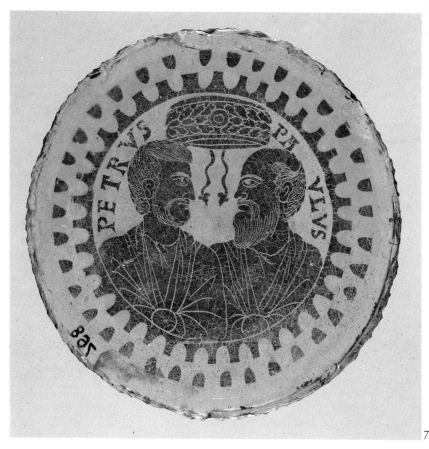

6 *Ivory from the Christian Museum of the Vatican Library. The first Christians often decorated their everyday objects with religious themes. This ivory, part of an oculist's case, illustrates the Healing of the man who was blind from birth, a symbol of conversion to the light of faith.*

7 *Gilded glass from the Christian Museum of the Vatican Library, with the two founders of the Church of Rome engraved in gold at the bottom of the cup. Other religious subjects often appear on these vessels, probably gifts exchanged among Christian friends.*

specific preacher brought the Gospel message to Rome, as was the case in many churches elsewhere — St. Paul would have mentioned it, especially if the evangelist had been St. Peter. Rather, Christianity seems to have sprung up spontaneously in the heart of the Roman Jewish community, which was largely composed of tradespeople whose contact with their homeland must have brought them early knowledge of the impact produced by the preaching of Jesus of

Nazareth and his followers. The book of The Acts of the Apostles mentions that there were "strangers of Rome" among those present on the first occasion the Apostles spoke in Jerusalem. It was almost certainly the ferment among the Jews of Rome, caused by conversions to the new doctrine, that set off the controversy and public unrest whose intensity finally led the Emperor Claudius to expel all Jews from the city in about AD 50. This is reported by the pagan writer, Suetonius, and the same story is told by St. Paul, who met exiles from the capital in Greece. But after the death of Claudius, when the exiles returned, they were already divided into two different religious beliefs and organizations. The Christian community had by now opened its doors to converts from paganism, and had prospered thereby, for new adherents came in a continuous stream from every strata of society. But this welcoming of the pagans collided with the rigidly exclusive tradition of the Judaic communities, even those of the Diaspora, and was almost certainly what caused the final separation of Christians from Jews, a development which took place in other cities as well.

The Christians of Rome were for the most part poor and humble folk. They generally lived in densely populated neighborhoods in the suburbs, especially near the sites which offered the possibility of a lively trade in supplies for the capital, or along the banks of the Tiber, or near industries like the transport services on the Appian Way. The army had shown itself from the start a favourable ground for the propagation of Christian ideas, and there were also many Christians among the workers in the field of entertainment — in the circuses, amphiteatres, theatres, and *naumachias* dedicated to the public spectacles which were so essential a part of Roman life. Many more were to be found among the masses of slaves — from the imperial palace and the rich patrician residences to the city at large, where they made up the swarms of public servants employed in construction work, in the maintenance of aqueducts, road and drainage systems, and in fire-fighting and street cleaning.
But there were also rich and powerful figures among the Christians of Rome. By the end of the first century even the niece of the Emperor Domitian, Flavia Domitilla, had been

5

8

9

8 Fossor, or gravedigger, at work, depicted in a painting from the Catacomb of Saints Marcellinus and Peter. The overwhelmingly vast necropoli of underground Rome are the creation of these humble workers, who opened galleries and cubicula, decorated them with frescoes and then buried the dead in them.

9 Banquet illustrated in a chamber of the catacomb of St. Callixtus. This ancient agape *funeral rite, formerly held to be a representation of the Eucharist, is a pagan ceremonial which symbolizes loving union with the dead. The Church treated this as a rite of love and charity and tolerated it until the fifth century.*

sentenced to exile as a Christian and had ended her life on the island of Ponza with a "*longum martyrium*", as St. Jerome says. Indeed, who but the wealthy could provide the economic means for organizing the Christian community? Believers gathered in their homes for the performance of eucharistic and baptismal rites, to receive religious instruction, and to assist the needy. During the third century a certain number of these rich homes became established centers of Christianity, much like modern parishes today. In the fourth century, there were twenty-five of them. Each of these "*tituli*", as they were called, bore the name of the owner, whom the civil authorities held juridically responsible for the property and all that went on in it. The gratitude of the Roman community was reflected in a long-cherished memory of these former benefactors, and when majestic churches later replaced the houses during the Reign of Peace, the original name was kept in nearly all of them. Throughout the fifth century, many of their former owners were even held to be saints by the populace, or were confused with martyrs bearing the same name: Sabina, Balbina, Cecilia, Anastasia, Grisogonus, Eusebius, Pudens. Archaeological excavations have only rarely revealed traces of these early household churches, and those which have been discovered lack any very evident signs of Christianity, like the *orant* (a figure with arms outstretched in prayer symbolizing the faithful) painted in a hall of the house discovered beneath the *titulus* of Bizans del Celio. Many factors contribute to explain this. The new church was not always built precisely on the site of the old *titulus*, but frequently on more suitable neighboring ground. Or the ancient parish center might have been located in an upper-story apartment, as still happens today in many of the city's suburbs. It is a well-known fact that the enormous population of the capital led residential Roman architecture to develop upwards, so that buildings in Rome, unlike the type of structure found in Pompeii and other cities, were up to four or five stories high. Obviously, the construction of titular basilicas towards the end of the fourth and during the fifth centuries resulted in the complete eradication of the memory of these ancient places of worship.

But the underground cemeteries still bear well-preserved traces of another aspect of the beneficence of wealthy Roman Christians towards their community: the donation of land for private burial grounds. The names of these cemeteries, like those of the urban *tituli*, reveal the generosity of the owners of the property in which they lie: Priscilla, Domitilla, Maximus, Thraso, Commodilla, Agnes, Ottavilla, etc. And in some of the catacombs of the pre-Constantinian period it is possible to distinguish original nuclei which were enlarged later to make room for many more graves than were necessary for the members of a single family. We have proof of Church possession, from the start, for one catacomb only, "the cemetery", as the author of the early third century *Philosophumena* calls

FIRMIA·VICTORA·QVE·VIXIT·ANNIS LXV

SEVERA INDEO VI VAS

it, where nearly all the popes of that century were buried. Its name today is St. Callixtus (Cf. p. 21). Perhaps there were other community areas as well, like the recently discovered Domitilla nucleus (Cf. p. 25), named after the Flavii Aurelii, but probably these, too, had their first origins in the beneficence of the wealthy, who granted the Church use of their lands as burial ground. With the passage of time, nearly all cemeteries became the property of the Church and were directly administered by it. But numerous exceptions still existed during the Reign of Peace: private cemeteries belonging to Christian families who preferred not to join the Church's funeral organization. An example was discovered on the Via Latina in 1956 (Cf. p. 33), a small *hypogeum* full of stupendous paintings — a regular fourth century pinacoteca!

The early beginnings of ecclesiastical organization date back to the time of Pope Fabian (236-50). He divided the city into seven districts and entrusted seven deacons with the supervision of the cultural, instructional and charitable activities that went on in the *tituli* of each. Another of their tasks was funeral organization, for which the state did not provide at that time, and each district was allotted a burial zone outside the walls, with a certain number of cemeteries. The plan in this volume shows their probable division.

Cemeteries were not built underground out of a desire for safety from

10 Bone doll, with articulated arms and legs, found in the lime used to seal a small loculus in the cemetery of Novatian. The children's tombs in the catacombs are often furnished with a profusion of decorative objects: lamps, vessels for perfumes, toys, bells, and other mementoes of those young creatures.

11 Epigraph with symbols from the Pio Christian Museum. The ship guided by the lighthouse beam on its journey towards the port symbolizes the journey towards salvation with faith as the guide.

12 Epitaph of Severa from the catacomb of Priscilla, now in the Vatican Museum. The inscription wishes the deceased a life in God, and she appears dressed in the palla signifying nobility. The Adoration of the Magi expresses her Christian faith.

13 Votive epigraph which the Deacon Gaudentius had painted on the tomb of the martyr Novatian. This is an example of the great care shown by Christians for the tombs of the heroes of the faith.

persecution, which is a romantic fantasy encouraged by the famous novels of the last century and still dear to the popular imagination today. The ancients willingly made use of underground land when it could be easily and safely excavated: from time immemorial the soft tufa of Latium had favored the development of a vast network of subterranean tunnels for waterworks, of chambers and galleries for graves, and even of recreation areas concealed in places called "cryptoporticus" beneath summer villas. The Christians and Jews of Rome simply found in the underground cemetery the solution to a problem which the large number of community members, and the choice of burial rather than cremation, had made increasingly difficult in a city where space was at a premium and suburban land was costly.

The multi-levelled network of catacomb galleries could be brought to a height of five meters with further digging, and offered room for thousands of tombs along the walls and in the ground. The simplest were the *loculi*, rectangular cavities dug one above the other in the tufa walls.

14

15

Each corpse was wrapped in a sheet before being placed in the tomb, which often contained two or more members of the same family. The name of the deceased was painted or sculpted on the brick or marble slab serving as its door, together with other pertinent information, usually the day and month of death. Small terracotta lamps and vases for perfume were often placed above the tomb, like the lights and flowers in cemeteries today. The sombre galleries lit by the dancing lamp flames must have made an impressive sight. A richer type of tomb was the *arcosolium*, a cell for the dead hollowed out of the tufa and often plastered and frescoed, with a horizontal slab for a lid over the grave surmounted by an arch. *Arcosolia* are most often found in *cubicula*, small rooms constituting family or corporation vaults. They are sometimes illuminated by pit-like openings in the vaulting resembling a skylight, which originally served for the removal of earth during the excavations.

The catacombs were used as cemeteries until the early fifth century. The colossal development of some of them was due to the cult of

14 Sarcophagus of Domitilla, now in the Vatican. Mid-fourth-century. Here we see the symbolism in artists' representations of the Passion at that time. At the center is the cross with the monogram of Christ and the crown of victory. To the right, Christ before Pilate; to the left, the Cyrenian and the coronation — but with laurel, not thorns.

15 Sarcophagus from the Vatican cemetery, fourth century. At the center, the Law being delivered to St. Peter, who symbolizes the authority of Christ the Lawgiver. Opposite Peter is Paul, shown in a gesture of approval and acclamation. At the far sides, two scenes in evident symbolic connection: the sacrifice of Isaac, and the beginning of Christ's ordeal before the tribunal of Pilate.

the martyrs, which led the faithful to seek burial closer to the sacred tombs as a near guarantee of salvation.

When burials there came to an end, the catacombs became sanctuaries. Immense numbers of pilgrims thronged to Rome, the Holy City, from every part of Europe. In spite of the

wars against the Goths in the sixth century, the Longobard raids of the seventh and the growing insecurity and poverty of the Roman countryside, the martyrs' sanctuaries were still regularly restored and embellished by the popes.

The *Itinerari*, guides for pilgrims written in the seventh and eighth centuries, show that devotion to them was still alive at that period. Nearly all of them were restored again in Pope Hadrian's time (772-95). But during the first decades of the ninth century, relics were transferred with even greater frequency from the original tombs to churches within the city walls. Each and every catacomb was thereby doomed to extinction, for the cult of the martyrs was the sole reason for continuing visits and regular restoration. The entrances to that underground world finally vanished beneath subsidences of the earth and an overgrowth of vegetation, and except for a few galleries, the catacombs remained unknown until the sixteenth century, when Antonio Bosio, "the Columbus of subterranean Rome" (1575-1629), began a systematic investigation. He located

about thirty catacombs, and after him the number of new discoveries slowly grew. Unfortunately, the pillage of marble and precious objects grew as well. But with the founding of the *Pontificia Commissione di Archeologia Sacra* in 1852, and De Rossi's extensive research which outlined a path for further study, the catacombs assumed their rightful place as the most stirring and popular of the monuments of Christian antiquity.

The most important of the Roman catacombs are illustrated in this volume with a well-paced and precise text by Fabrizio Mancinelli, who provides notes on the collection prepared by Professor Josi and shown here in Mauro Sarri's splendid photographs, taken for the Istituto Fotografico Editoriale Scala of Florence. He also provides brief additional comments to introduce the principal buildings of the cult — those which, during the Reign of Peace, lent to the capital of the Empire its new face as capital of the Christian world.

Rome, March 8, 1980

16, 17 *The Flavian amphiteatre, one of the most prestigious places of entertainment ever built. The Roman passion for ''ludi'', or games held in circus and amphiteatre, was truly incredible. After the famous fire of 64, Nero's repression of Christianity took the form of cruel spectacles given in the Circus of Caligula in the Vatican. Even in the persecutions that followed, martyrs frequently performed their sacrifice in places of entertainment — more often in the Circus Maximus than in the Colosseum. For example, we know that when crucifixions took place, the crosses were often planted along the spine, a long wall of earth which divided the arena at the center.*

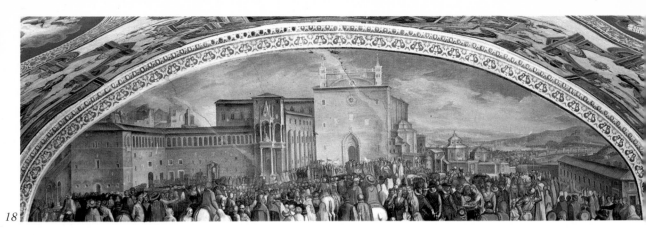

St. John Lateran

The basilica of St. John Lateran was the first large Christian place of worship to be built within the city walls. Constantine, the emperor whose Edict of 313 granted the Christians freedom of worship, chose to erect the basilica on this site near the Laterani family residence, first of all because it belonged to him — in fact, the *equites singulares*, private guard of the Emperor, had their barracks there —, and secondly because its distance from the Forum would be less likely to irritate non-Christians. The basilica, which rises on the ruins of earlier structures, including the barracks of the *equites singulares*, was begun between 313 and 314 under the pontificate of either Pope Melchiades (311-14) or Pope Sylvester (314-35) and was dedicated to the Savior. The dedication to John the baptist and St. John the Evangelist was a later addition by Gregory the Great (590-604). In the north-north-east area to the right of the basilica stood the patriarchate, residence of the pope as Bishop of Rome. The baptistery was built behind the apse, to the north west. It was the only one in existence in Constantine's time, and once a year, at Easter, the pope administered baptism there.

The basilica's appearance today differs from its early Christian form, although Borromini's baroque restructuring of the naves between 1646 and 1650, commissioned by Innocent X, substantially reflects the proportions and distribution of light and space in the Constantinian basilica (*20*). The old edifice, like the present one, was built on a basilical plan with five aisles (*21*), and was

53.73 meters wide and about 30 meters high. The width of the central nave was 18.73 meters and its length 90.55 meters. It ended in a 9.22 meters deep semicircular apse pierced by ample windows, and was separated from the side aisles by a row of nineteen red granite columns with beams above. It had a truss-beam roof, perhaps left visible. Light filtered through a series of rectangular arch centred windows. The inner aisles — 7.94 meters wide and 90.23 meters long — were lower, and took their lighting from a series of crescent windows; a row of twenty-one antique green marble columns set on high bases and connected by arches divided them from the outer aisles. These were even lower and less well-lighted, and much shorter (74.88 meters), although of almost the same width (7.69 meters). They ended in two rooms, 8.93 meters by 11.45 meters, which projected slightly on the outside, and formed a sort of small nave transept. The basilica walls were probably covered with marble and decorated with paintings at window level. The floor of the central nave was antique gold marble, and the basin of the apse was covered in gold leaf.

No visible traces remain of the Constantinian patriarchate. The present Lateran Palace was built in the days of Sixtus V (1585-90), as was the *Scala Santa* edifice. However, the latter includes Early Christian structures — such as the *scrinium* with a sixth- to seventh-century fresco representing St. Augustine — as well as medieval structures like the thirteenth-century chapel of the *Sancta Sanctorum*. The adjoining Leonine *Triclinium* is the architect Ferdinando Fuga's reconstruction (1743) of the dining-room of the medieval patriarchate, built

and decorated by Leo III (795-816). The structure of today's Baptistery (*19*), on the other hand, is still essentially Early Christian. Its original plan was certainly round. The octagonal plan of the present edifice — about 20 meters in diameter — is the result of restoration work ordered by Sixtus III (432-40). Inside, eight porphyry columns with beams above separate the central hall from the ring-shaped chamber, once covered by a barrel vault, which surrounds it. There was originally a dome over the central hall, and eight semicircular windows for illumination. The present-day *tiburio* dates from a restoration by Paul III in 1540. In front of Sixtus III's edifice was an atrium in the shape of a forceps, now known as the chapel of either St. Secunda and St. Rufina or St. Cyprian and St. Justin, with marble and mosaic ornamentations, partly still in place. It had a beam-roofed portico supported by two porphyry columns. The chapels of St. John the Baptist and of St. John the Evangelist, standing one to the right, the other to the left of the actual entrance, were built during the papacy of St. Hilary (461-67). The vault of the latter still has the mosaic decoration of that time, with the Mystical Lamb at its center. The chapel of St. Venantius came later. It was built by Pope John IV (640-42) and decorated by Pope Theodore (642-48).

21 Plan of the basilica of St. John Lateran. The structure of the present basilica is shown in black, the foundations of the Constantinian edifice are outlined in brown.

19 Baptistery of St. John Lateran. Founded with the basilica, it stands on the remains of a villa of the first century A.D., and of a later thermal structure.

20 Filippo Gagliardi, fresco showing the interior of St. John Lateran, 1651, Church of S. Martino ai Monti. It provides a reconstruction of the original Constantinian basilica, albeit with a few inaccuracies, such as the arches connecting the central nave, columns instead of beams, and ogival windows in the central nave.

20

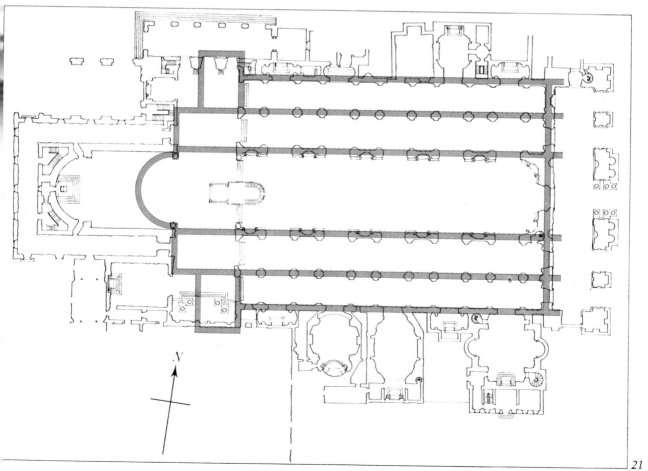

N

21

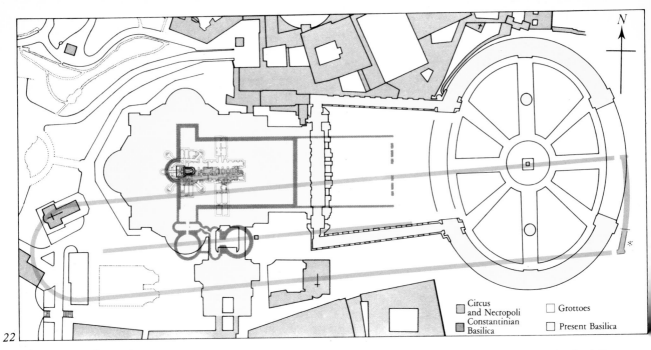

St. Peter's

* Wall of the «carceres», the starting point for quadriga chariot races, now in the subterranean portion of the Palazzo delle Congregazioni Romane. The visible part is 17.45 meter long.

Circus and Necropoli
Constantinian Basilica
Grottoes
Present Basilica

The basilica of St. Peter was erected by the Emperor Constantine and Pope Sylvester to preserve the tomb of the Prince of the Apostles, over which a commemorative monument called the Trophy of Gaius had been built towards the middle of the second century. The memorial was called a "trophy" because the word reflected the Early Christian belief that the saint's martyrdom was a victory of faith over death. The site was part of a pagan necropolis located on the slopes of *Mons Vaticanus*, not far from the Circus of Gaius and Nero where, according to tradition, the apostle was martyred in AD 64. The necropolis (*22*) extended along the north side of the circus, from east to west. During the first and second centuries numerous tombs were built (*23*), some of them Christian, and all with south entrances facing the circus. They belonged to the families of wealthy freedmen — the Aelii, the Aurelii, the Caetenni, the Julii, the Marcii, the Tullii, the Ulpii, and the Falerii. Some of these originally pagan structures were later decorated by Christians, for example the Mausoleum of the Julii, seen and described for the first time by the chronicler, Tiberio Alfarano, in 1574. In the center of its vault is a mosaic representing Jesus as the Sun God (*24*), and on its walls one can still

make out images whose connotations are clearly Christian.

From the end of the second century, the tombs continued to spread southwards until they covered the axis of the circus, which had by then fallen into disuse. The most imposing of them, was a rotunda with a forceps-shaped atrium in front, perhaps the first of its kind. It stood only a few meters to the west of the circus obelisk (removed by Sixtus V to St. Peter's Square in 1586) and was aligned with it. Consecrated under Pope Symmachus (498-515) and dedicated to St. Andrew, it was later connected with the nearby mausoleum of Honorius at the southern extremity of the transept of the Constantinian basilica. Both of these mausoleums were originally destined to be the imperial family tombs of Theodosius. The Trophy of Gaius took its name from the presbyter who mentioned it for the first time in 200. It stood in the north-western zone of the necropolis, in an open space (Camp P) measuring approximately 7 meters by 4 meters; it was surrounded by mausoleums and sepulchral ground and bounded on the west by a red plaster-covered wall (*27*).

The monument, in the shape of an aedicula, was built at the same time as the red wall, and consisted of two niches excavated in the wall itself and

a third, invisible, underground niche communicating with the tomb of the apostle. The two upper niches were separated by a slab of travertine, 1.80 meters wide, resting on two small columns in front. The lower one survives in today's "Niche of the Sacred Pallia", but the upper one, which had at its center a small embrasure communicating with the outside, and may have been crowned by a tympanum, has perished with time. The entire monument was approximately 2.30 meters high. During the third century, two small walls were added to the north and south of the lower niche. The north wall has graffiti with invocations to the apostle. The niche and the floor in front of it were covered with marble, and the open space with a mosaic.

The basilica was built between 321 and about 329 to create a monumental setting dedicated to the memory of the apostle, and to favor the growth of his cult among the great mass of believers. In order to create a platform for the building, the Constantinian architects had to bury the necropolis and dig out part of the hill to the north. In front of the basilica stood a large rectangular atrium with porticoes inside, on the entrance side of the church façade. In the center of the courtyard was the fountain with the bronze pinecone, now to be seen in the Vatican Palace courtyard which bears its name. It was protected by a bronze canopy supported by four porphyry columns and crowned by a variety of objects, including the two bronze peacocks currently on display in the new wing of the Vatican Museum.

Inside the basilica were five aisles separated by twenty-two columns of various colors, with a beamed roof in the central nave and connecting arches in the side aisles. Like their bases and capitals these were spoil taken from more ancient buildings. The five aisles led to the transept, and then to the apse, with St. Peter's funeral monument (28) dominant at the center. A marble parallelepiped set off the second-century aedicula, visible through a double door in it on the nave side. This coffer-like structure sat upon a marble-covered platform which was raised a step higher than the transept floor. Above it was a bronze canopy supported by four twisted columns. Beam work connected them to two more twisted columns situated at the very end of the apse, which contained a basin covered with gold leaf. The Constantinian columns survive in the present basilica, beside the niches in the cupola pillars dedicated to St. Longinus, St. Andrew, St. Helen and St. Veronica.

The central nave was better lit than the other aisles, thanks to eleven windows in the upper part of both its walls and a double row of windows in

23

24

25

26

25 St. Peter's, Treasury. Sarcophagus of Junius Bassus, fourth century. Above, center, the "Traditio Legis"; below, the entrance into Jerusalem. The other episodes are, above, the Sacrifice of Abraham, the Capture of St. Peter, the Capture of Christ, and Christ before Pilate; below, Job, Adam and Eve, Daniel in the Lion's Den, and St. Paul led to his martyrdom. The artist clearly intended to unite the supreme sacrifice of the fathers of the Roman Church and the Passion of Christ. The same concept inspires basilica construction from the end of the fourth century on, so that the symbolic place of Jesus' sacrifice — the altar — stands right over the tomb of the martyr, or includes part of his relics.

26 St. Peter's, Grottoes. Sarcophagus of Probus, end of fourth century. In the central niche, a beardless Christ with the jewelled cross in His right hand and a scroll in His left stands on a hill from which issue the four rivers of Paradise. Saints Peter and Paul are to the side. In the side niches are the other apostles in groups of two.

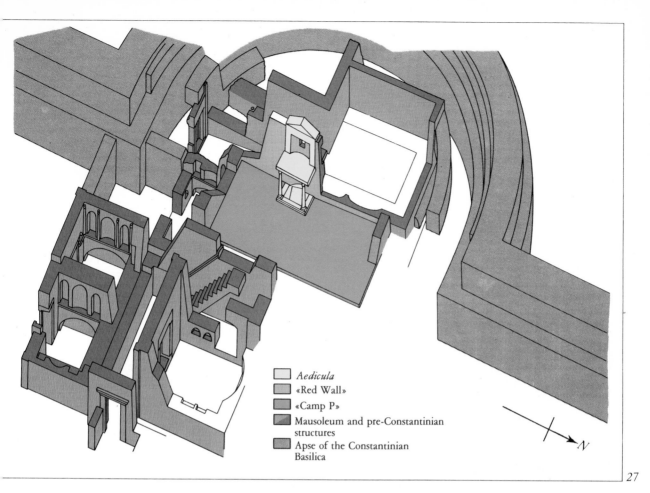

Aedicula
«Red Wall»
«Camp P»
Mausoleum and pre-Constantinian structures
Apse of the Constantinian Basilica

N

27

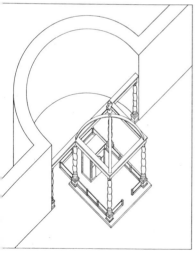

27 Reconstruction of Camp P. The spot over St. Peter's tomb in the necropolis was marked by a monument, in the shape of an aedicula, located in the so-called Camp P, a cemetery zone which was bounded to the west by the "red wall" containing the monument niches. The plan of the basilica had the monument situated on the chord of the apse (from Apollony Ghetti).

28 Reconstruction of the apse of the Constantinian basilica. (from Toynbee - Ward Perkins).

29

29 Ivory Pola casket with the Constantinian arrangement of the tomb of St. Peter (Venice, Archaeological Museum).

30

31

30 *Domenico Tasselli, Interior of the Constantinian basilica of St. Peter's. Detached fresco, formerly in the Vatican Grottoes, now in the Sacristy.*

31 *Domenico Tasselli, Drawing with the atrium and façade of the Constantinian basilica of St. Peter's, about 1611. Biblioteca Apostolica Vaticana.*

the façade. It ended in a triumphal arch at the transept, whereas the side aisles had only two columns with beams between. The roof over the central nave was pitched to both sides and over the two side aisles towards the outer side only. The transept, an entity apart from the rest of the church, served as a *martyrium*. It was lower than the central nave, ending

with exedrae both to the north and to the south. These were lower than the transept, and they projected beyond the walls of the nave and aisles.

The basilica designed by the Constantinian architects had various functions: it was an assembly hall for the resident population, a *martyrium*, a church and object of pilgrimages, a covered cemetery and, finally, a hall for banquet and funeral libations. It had no fixed altar. The first altar dates back to the time of Gregory the Great, who raised the presbytery thus concealing the tomb of the apostle in the crypt below. The faithful had a sign of its presence however, in the ciborium and in the altar, which was placed directly above the tomb.

The basilica of St. Peter was larger than that of St. John. The atrium was 90.92 meters deep and its width the same as that of the church, 63.42 meters. The central nave was 90.9? meters long and 25.15 meters wide and the side aisles had the following widths: 9.49 meters (outer south aisle), 9.78 meters (inner south aisle), 9.79 meters (inner north aisle), 9.2? meters (outer north aisle). The transept measured 66.43 meters by 16.82, the exedrae 10.76 meters by 16.82. The church height at the façade was about 38.48 meters, but the transept was little more than 2? meters high. Today the only remains of the original basilica are to be found in the so-called Vatican Grottoes, which are level with the floor of the Constantinian edifice, and in the necropolis below it. Nevertheless a fairly accurate picture can be formed from various ancient illustrations. In the ivory bas-relief of the Pola casket dating from about 430, the Constantinian disposition of the monument to the apostle (*29*) appears with great clarity. A sixteenth century fresco by Domenico Tasselli (*30*) shows a vertical section of the church, with the naves ending in the so-called "dividing wall", erected in 1538 so that religious functions could go on while the new building was under construction. Finally, a drawing by Tasselli (*31*), dated about 1611, illustrates the exterior of the old basilica, with the atrium, the pinecone fountain and the façade.

32

n Sebastiano

ne church of San Sebastiano, once
usilica apostolorum, stands on the
gh-hand side of the Appian Way
3), about two kilometers from the
orta San Sebastiano (*32*). On the
her side of the road, slightly further
uth, are the Circus of Maxentius
d his son, Romulus', tomb. In an-
:nt times this spot was a deep
·llow, used as a pozzolana stone
uarry and dubbed *ad catacumbus*, a
rm which in modern times has
me to be a synonym for "under-
·ound cemetery". The catacomb of
. Sebastian originated in the
·lleries of the abandoned pit pro-
·bly as early as the first century, and
·s developed towards the north and
·st mainly during the third century.
·e oldest building in the area was a
·la constructed during the first cen-
·ry, to the west of the pit. It had a
·arly square plan, and the rooms
·re arranged on two stories around a
·ntral courtyard. The entrance faced
·st onto a small street, parallel to

the Appian Way. Another similar,
but later, edifice found under the
basilica, the so-called *Villa Piccola*,
contains geometric decorations
characteristic of the wall painting of
the time (*38*). Along the north wall
of the first villa and beyond it, at the
edge of the hollow, were a series of
mausoleums also from the first century. They lined the sides of a small
street in a double file.

Towards the middle of the second
century, the bottom of the hollow
was earthed over to create a small
level open space, about 9 meters
below the present church floor. On
one side of it three mausoleums (*35*)
were built in succession. The oldest
is probably the one called the
"mausoleum of the axe". Shortly
before 260 — perhaps in 258 — the
clearing was covered with enough
earth to raise the ground level by
about 6 meters. On this new open
area the *memoria* of St. Peter and St.
Paul was built, bounded on the north
by the row of first-century mausoleums, and on the west by the villa.
The complex was on a trapezoidal
plan, and extended 23 meters from

*32 Porta San Sebastiano and the
Aurelian Walls.*

east to west and 18 meters from
north to south. It was essentially
a brick-paved courtyard with two
covered loggias all along the northern
and eastern sides. A steep stairway
in the center led down to an underground spring which supplied the
water necessary for the *refrigeria*, or
funeral libations. The eastern loggia,
known as the *triclia*, was raised 1.15
meters above the courtyard pavement. Its walls were decorated with
flowers, birds and animals in fresco,
but there is barely a trace of them left
today. Instead, numerous graffiti
(*34*) have been found with invocations to the Apostles, Peter and Paul.
The entry faced east, towards the Appian Way, which was about sixty
meters away. In the northwest corner
of the courtyard the real *memoria*
stood (*36*), its lower portion consisting of a small southwards facing
niche, with two terracotta columns
beside it stuccoed and painted to look
like marble. The upper part of the

monument has been destroyed and cannot be reconstructed. In the opposite wall of the courtyard, not far from the southwest corner, was the so-called "delta-cell", a rectangular exedra with an apse and two columns in front of it. Its original function is unclear, but eventually it, too, was used as a mausoleum.

The Early Christian basilica (37) differed enormously from the present day church, which acquired its new appearance during the seventeenth century. It was built during the first half of the fourth century on the area comprising the *memoria* and the preexisting necropolis. Experts are not in agreement about the date of its construction, but it was built somewhere between 310 and 350. Perhaps it was begun under Maxentius. If so, it would be the prototype for the Constantinian basilicas of Sant'Agnese (Cf. p. 49), San Lorenzo and Santi Marcellino e Pietro (Cf. p. 39). It had the same east-west axis as the *memoria* and consisted of a central nave, flanked by two small side aisles joined by an ambulatory in the apse to the west, and at the entrance, to the east. The U-shape of the whole resembled that of a circus. A row of pillars with connecting arches separated the central naves from the side aisles. Ample arch windows lighted the central nave, which had a truss-beam roof and was 58.30 meters long and 13.50 meters wide. The 7-meter wide side aisles and ambulatory received less light. The total length of the interior was 73.40 meters.

A large rectangular courtyard without porticoes connected the basilica with the Appian Way. The initial absence of a pavement in both the central nave and side aisles is easily explained by the earlier use of the edifice as burial place. It seems that at least the *triclia* portion of the third century *memoria* was visible at first. It was located in the eastern part of the central nave, where the basilica and *triclia* were on the same level, about two meters below the western part, which in turn was just about level with what is now the church floor. Only afterwards, when the *memoria* was completely buried, was the floor uniformly raised to its present level. The crypt of St. Sebastian probably antedates the construction of the church, and must have originated with the enlargement of the first century gallery of the catacomb, which

33 *View of the Roman pavement of the Appian Way, along which many important catacombs are found.*

34 *Catacomb of St. Sebastian. Third century graffiti in the "triclia" beneath the basilica, with invocations to the apostles Peter and Paul.*

18

grew enormously during the centuries that followed. The entrance to the catacomb, no different today from what it was during the Middle Ages, is through a room which has always contained the tomb of the saint to whom the church was eventually dedicated. Outstanding among the numerous mausoleums lining the southern flank of the basilica and all erected in the fourth century is the rotunda of the Uranii (about 349). The Platonia mausoleum lies at the very end of the group, to the west. Tradition had it that this mausoleum was built by Pope Damasus (366-84) in honor of the Prince of the Apostles and decorated with the *platoma*, a marble slab mentioned in the *Liber pontificalis*.

35

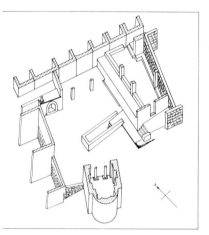

35 *Catacomb of St. Sebastian. View of the three mausoleums.*

36a-36b Reconstruction (from Tolotti) and model (from Pacini) of the "memoria" of St. Sebastian.

37

37 *Model of the old Early Christian basilica of St. Sebastian (from Pacini). The two side naves were join-* *ed by an ambulatory. This was a typical architectural feature of Constantinian temples.*

38 Catacomb of St. Sebastian. Wall decoration of the ''Villa Piccola'', about 230-240. This is a typical example of the stylized decoration of the period, in which the architectonic elements of the Pompeian style are reduced to mere graphic notation.

39 Catacomb of St. Sebastian. Fresco with bird and fruit-bowl in the Mausoleum of Marcus Clodius Hermes.

Catacomb of St. Callixtus

The catacomb of St. Callixtus (Via Appia Antica, 102) is the oldest official cemetery of the Christian community of Rome. The complex originated in an outdoor burial area which, according to Giovan Battista De Rossi, belonged to the Cecili family. It was named after the deacon Callixtus, who was appointed head of the cemetery under Pope Zephyrinus (199-217) and who, when he was himself pope (217-22), enlarged it greatly. No less than nine third-

century popes were buried here, in a crypt whose name reflects the fact. At certain points the cemetery complex is developed on as many as five levels, and its galleries spread over a distance of more than ten kilometers. The oldest part, situated to the right of the Appian Way as you leave Rome, contains second-century paintings. The catacomb of St. Callixtus, like the other catacombs, lay forgotten for a long while; the memory of where it stood was lost soon after the relics of

the martyrs had been transferred to churches within the city and the Appia Ardeatina *memoria* removed to St. Sebastian's — the one place that people continued to visit.

St. Callixtus was discovered accidentally by De Rossi during a visit to the Vigna Amendola in 1849. From several fragments of Pope Cornelius' epitaph (251-53), which he found there, he was able to identify the so-called Lucina district; Pius IX purchased the vineyard immediately,

41

42

41 Catacomb of St. Callixtus. Gallery with loculi.

42 Catacomb of St. Callixtus. Epitaph of Deacon Severus, in which it is written that this cleric, with the authorization of Pope Marcellinus (296-304), had a double cubiculum with an arcosolium and a skylight built to serve as tomb for himself and his family. The inscription also alludes to the resurrection of the dead: Young Severa will lie in this house of peace until the Lord restores to her body its immortal soul.

and De Rossi continued excavations. In 1854, he unearthed the Crypt of the Popes (40), containing the tombs of nine Pontiffs who reigned between 230 and 283: St. Pontian (230-35), St. Anterus (236), St. Fabian (236-50), St. Lucius I (253-54), St. Stephen I (254-57), St. Sixtus II (257-58), St. Dionysius (259-68), St. Felix I (269-74) and St. Eutychian (275-83); and in 1856 he uncovered Deacon Severus' chamber. Beside the popes lie three African bishops who died during a journey to Rome: Urban, Numidian and Octatus. The plan of the crypt is rectangular. A skylight provides illumination, and loculi and niches for sarcophagi line the side walls. On the rear wall, a marble slab reconstructed by De Rossi bears an ode written by Pope Damasus (366-84) in honor of the martyrs and bishops there laid to rest. In the cubiculum that Deacon Severus had erected for himself and his family with the permission of Pope Marcellinus (296-304), there is a marble *transenna* or screen which has an inscription (42) containing the very first reference to the Bishop of Rome as "Pope" (298). Opposite Deacon Severus' cubiculum is the cubiculum of the five saints (43) with a fresco (44) showing six figures in a garden full of flowers, their arms outstretched in the typical attitude of prayer. Each figure has his name inscribed at his side with the greeting "in peace". The fresco may be dated from the beginning of the fourth century, and in it the so-called compendium technique was used for the figures, each one taking shape with only a few, essential strokes of the brush.

One of the oldest nuclei of the St. Callixtus cemetery complex is the crypt of Lucina, where De Rossi found the traces which led him to discover the rest of the catacomb. Pope Cornelius lies here. He died in exile in Civitavecchia, and was removed to St. Callixtus' afterwards. On his tomb is the appellation "martyr", a later addition. The painting decorating the crypt shows the Good Shepherd (45), an allusion to Christ; it is an early third century work, executed with a very rapid compendium technique. Also part of the original cemetery was the cubicula of the Sacraments, so-called because they are decorated with paintings alluding to the Baptism and the

Eucharist. Among the many subjects depicted in these frescoes, which date from the first half of the third century, are the stories of Jonah, the Miracle of the Spring in the Desert, the Evangelical Fisherman, the Banquet of the Seven Disciples at Lake Tiberias, the Healing of the Paralytic, the Baptism of Jesus, Abraham's sacrifice, and a Eucharistic Banquet (46) in which fish and several baskets pointing at the Miracle of the Loaves and Fishes are shown beside a table with seven figures.

43 Catacomb of St. Callixtus. Cubiculum of the Five Saints. In fact, in this fresco there are six praying figures. They are shown in a garden, which symbolizes the abode of eternal happiness — parádeisos is the Greek term for garden. Beside each figure is a name: Dionysia, Nemesius, Procopius, Eliodora, Zoe, Arcadia.

44 Catacomb of St. Callixtus. Detail of a praying figure in the cubiculum of the Five Saints: Dionysas in pace.

45

45 *Catacomb of St. Callixtus. Fresco with the Good Shepherd in the crypt of Lucina.*

46 *Catacomb of St. Callixtus. Eucharistic banquet in the crypt of the Sacraments. The scene represented in this illustration could hardly be taken for a simple pagan funeral meal. It appears in several places in the Roman catacombs; and although it varies in form, it always contains the symbolic number of baskets filled with bread, a detail which is lacking in frescoes which clearly depict a* refrigerium, *or funeral banquet. The baskets commemorate the miracle wrought by Jesus in the desert, when he provided bread for the famished multitude. In the Gospel according to Saint John, in the famous discourses on the bread of heaven which abideth unto eternal life, this miracle is explicitly connected with the Eucharist. The other part of that rite is represented by a catacomb painter in the near-by crypt of Lucina, where a glass of red wine has been set among the loaves in the symbolic basket.*

46

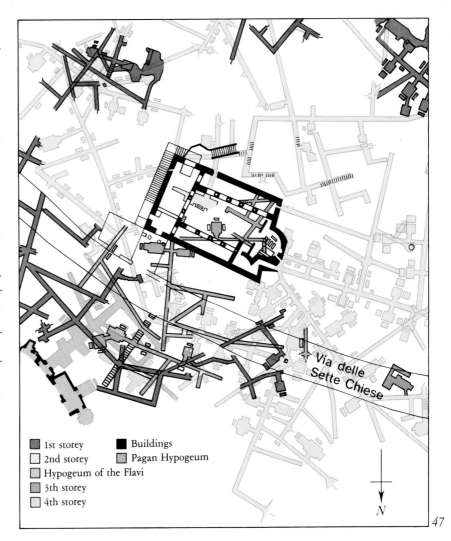

1st storey	Buildings
2nd storey	Pagan Hypogeum
Hypogeum of the Flavi	
3th storey	
4th storey	

Via delle Sette Chiese

N

47

Catacomb of Domitilla

One of the most extensive underground cemeteries in Rome, the catacomb of Domitilla originated with the establishment of several small cemeteries on lands belonging to Flavia Domitilla and given by her to her freedmen. Its entrance lies between Piazza dei Navigatori and the beginning of Via Ardeatina. Flavia Domitilla, niece of Flavius Clemens, consul in AD 95, was indirectly related to the imperial family, for her uncle had married Domitilla, niece of Vespasian. Her Christian faith led Domitian to exile her on the island of Ponza, where she died.

The catacomb was developed mainly on two levels — only rarely is there a third or fourth story of galleries and cubicula (47). The earliest Christian nucleus dates from the latter half of the second century. Between the end of the third century and the begin-

ning of the fourth, the bodies of the martyrs Nereus and Achilleus were placed in a crypt on the third level. It was transformed by Pope Damasus (366-84) into a small masonry basilica, and enlarged to its present size (31 meters long and from 17 to 12 meters wide) (48) between 390 and 395 by Pope Siricius. At the end of the fourth century, the basilica — which has now been rebuilt along the essential lines of the original — had its upper part projecting above the ground, and its floor on the level of the second story of the catacomb. A narthex stood in front of the main edifice, which had three aisles separated by two rows of four columns with connecting arches; the columns were plundered from other buildings, as were their capitals. The central nave, about 20 meters long and from 8.50 to 10 meters wide, rose above side aisles 3.50 to 4 meters in width: its illumination came from two rows of wide centered arch windows, and it ended in an apse to the

west. There were probably *matronei*, or women's galleries, above the side aisles. The altar area was bounded by a series of *transennae*, and a marble ciborium set off the altar, which was placed over the martyrs' tomb. Of the ciborium, only the supporting columns remain, with St. Achilleus' martyrdom depicted on one of them. The entry to the basilica of Saints Nereus and Achilleus was up a stairway leading to a side door in the narthex, just as it is today. During the eighth century, the building was stripped of everything that could be carried away, including the flooring, and afterwards the whole structure collapsed — perhaps as a result of the earthquake of 897. It was unearthed during excavations in 1873-74. In a small cubiculum, dug out right behind the apse of the basilica, is the arcosolium of the Veneranda (49), containing evidence that the cult of St. Petronilla had a following in the catacomb (in fact, the martyr's tomb may not be far from this cell): the

48

49

50

fresco on the rear lunette, painte
after 356, shows the decease
Veneranda being led into the garde
of paradise by a young maiden, iden
tified in script as St. Petronilla.
A large staircase linking the first an
second levels of the catacomb wa
discovered in 1854. On its wall
fresco (52), dating from about th
middle of the third century, shows
young shepherd holding a panpip
— a primitive wind instrument — i
his hand, surrounded by his flocks c

51

52

heep and rams, with four hills nclosing the scene in the backround. The figure symbolizes Christ, he Good Shepherd of the parable John 10, 1-16), as described on the ippus of Bishop Abercius now displayed in the Lateran Museum. The andscape in the illustration is evi-ence of this source: ''The holy shep-erd who leads his flocks to pasture n the mountains and in the valley''.

51 Catacomb of Domitilla. The Good Shepherd. There are other frescoes, similar to this one, in the same area, but in them a praying figure is shown behind each of the sheep in the garden. The allusion to the symbolic meaning of the scene is evident: the Good Shepherd is Christ leading the souls of the saved to the land of eternal happiness.

52 Catacomb of Domitilla. Christ as Orpheus. The shepherd with a pan-pipe in his hand and his flock of sheep about him has been inter-preted as Orpheus, the hero of pagan mythology whose sweet voice soothed even wild beasts, here depicted as a symbol of Christ, whose doctrine could move even the hardest of hearts.

27

53

54

53 *Catacomb of Priscilla. Scen*
from the life of a deceased woman
the chamber of the "Velatio".

54 *Catacomb of Priscilla. The thre*
children in the fiery furnace in th
chamber of the "Velatio".

55 *Catacomb of Priscilla. The "Cap*
pella Greca", or cubiculum of th
"Fractio panis".

Catacomb of Priscilla

Located at 430 Via Salaria, this two-level catacomb was probably named after Priscilla of the Acilii, a senatorial family whose name appears in one of the inscriptions in the Acili hypogeum on the first level. It differs from the other catacombs in its origins, for it grew up on the site of an *arenarium*, or pozzolana stone quarry, which had been abandoned after its entrance was blocked by a slide on the Via Salaria side. Christians began using the ample and irregular galleries on the first floor of the catacomb towards the beginning of the third century. They built about twenty tombs and niches, and

hollowed hundreds of loculi out of the walls, but most of these were later hidden by masonry added to prevent the walls caving in. The oldest sepulchres are on this level, including the Acili hypogeum and the so-called "*Cappella greca*" (55), built before the end of the second century.

The chapel is a rectangular chamber divided by a large arch into two spans, the second having three great niches in its walls. It was named "Greek Chapel" from the two Greek inscriptions in the right-hand niche, with dedications by a certain Obrinus to his cousin and companion Palladius, and to his wife, Nestoriana.

Against the left-hand wall is a lon masonry bench. The second centur decoration consists of ornament frescoes and biblical subjects cover ing the ceiling vault and the uppe part of the walls, and stucco pane with marbled painting below. O the arch in the first span is the Adora tion of the Magi (Matthew, 2), sym bol of the foundation of the church The oldest of all known illustration of the Virgin with Child appear there as well. On the entrance wa are the three Hebrews in the Fier Furnace (Daniel 3, 15-24; 43-50) the symbol of faith, and Mose bringing forth water from the roc

Exodus, 17, 6), a prefiguration of the Baptism. On the side walls are the Healing of the Sick of the Palsy (Matthew 9, 2; Mark 2, 2; Luke 5, 18), a symbol of penitence, and the stories of Susanna (Daniel, 13), which symbolize faith in God in the face of persecution and affliction: the perfidious elders are shown on the left attempting to ensnare the unfortunate Susanna, while on the right Susanna and Daniel offer up their thanks to God. Further on, next to the entrance wall, is the phoenix dying in the flames, symbol of the resurrection of the body, and above it a head crowned with garlands of wheat representing summer. The paintings in the second span represent Daniel in the Lion's Den (Daniel 6, 31) on the right, Abraham's sacrifice (Genesis 22, 9-10) on the left, and on the dividing arch the resurrection of Lazarus (John 11, 44). Above the apse niche is the Eucharistic banquet, the most important theme from an iconographical point of view. Sitting at the table are seven persons, among them a woman with veiled head. At the far left, a bearded figure, dressed in tunic and pallium, extends his arm to break the bread (*fractio panis*). On the table before him are a chalice of wine, a plate with two fishes, and one with five loaves of bread. The composition is bordered by seven baskets of bread, three to one side, four to the other. The chapel faces onto the so-called *cryptoporticus* or underground portico, a vast area with a rectangular plan and a cross-vault ceiling in masonry, like the walls. Another interesting burial chamber, built after the chapel, is the cubiculum of the Velati, decorated with paintings from the second half of the third century. Its name comes from a fresco on the back wall showing scenes from the life of the deceased (*53*), who appears in the center with his arms raised in an attitude of prayer. (At his feet is the signature of an illustrious later visitor, Antonio Bosio (1575-1629), who discovered the Roman catacombs and published the first scientific studies of them). On the left a bishop gives his blessing at the dead man's wedding, while the youth at his side hands him the nuptial veil (*flammeum*); the scroll in the bride's hands is the *tabula nuptialis*, a document enumerating marital duties. The woman as mother is shown on

55

the right with a baby in her arms, a group which was thought in the past to represent the Madonna and Child. On the wall to the left of the *Velatio* fresco is the Sacrifice of Abraham (Genesis 22, 9-10), and on the wall to the right (*54*) are the three Hebrews in the Fiery Furnace (Daniel 3, 19-26), another most interesting iconographical representation; in it a dove appears with a branch in its beak as symbol of divine intervention. The vault has a painting of the Good Shepherd at the center and a cycle of stories of Jonah (Jonah 1, 1-15).

Many popes were buried on the first level of the catacomb: Marcellinus (296-304), Marcellus I (308-09), and Sylvester (314-35) who lies in the small *ad corpus* basilica he had built over the tomb of St. Felix and St. Philip; Liberius (352-56), Siricius (384-99), Celestine I (422-32) and Vigilius (537-55) as well. The second

level is quite different in character, for its galleries, unlike the casually winding passageways of the first, were designed in accordance with a precise plan: it has two long parallel galleries with ramifications in a fishbone pattern, and the original entrance was above ground through two large stairways. The four underground connections between the galleries of the two stories are later additions. Many saints also rest in this catacomb. Among them are Pudenziana and Prassede who, according to tradition, were daughters of Pudens and contemporaries of the apostles, and Aquila and Prisca, the couple often mentioned by St. Paul, who were the titulars of the Church on the Aventine hill.

56 *Catacomb of Commodilla. Th[e] basilica of Saint Felix and Sai[nt] Adauctus. The two martyrs are po[r]trayed on the central tomb, and the[y] appear six times more in fresco[es] decorating other parts of th[e] catacomb as well. Saint Luke, th[e] evangelist, is painted on the pillar [to] the right, with a surgical instrumen[t] bag hanging from his right arm. Th[is] is the first time that the saint is po[r]trayed with doctor's insignia. Th[e] fresco dates from the reign of th[e] Byzantine Emperor Constantine I[V] (668-685) according to an inscriptio[n] in the border which frames th[e] figure.*

57 *Catacomb of Commodill[a] cubiculum of an employee of th[e] "annona" — the revenue and foo[d] supplies administration —, who[se] name was Leo. Bust of Christ. La[te] fourth-early fifth century. This [is] among the first of the bearded im[-]ages of Christ.*

Catacomb of Commodilla

Rediscovered in 1903 by the *Pontificia Commissione di Archeologia Sacra* (Papal Commission of Sacred Archaeology) — it had first been sighted in 1720 — this catacomb is located at 42 Via delle Sette Chiese and takes its name from the owner of the land, the matron Commodilla. The martyrs Felix and Adauctus, Merita and Nemesius are buried here. Felix was a priest. He was being led to the place appointed for his death when Adauctus, a stranger, came to meet him, and declared himself a Christian. For this, he was put to death with the priest. The crypt of

these martyrs, at the foot of the original entrance stairway, was built during the Pontificate of Siricius (384-99), who enlarged a pre-existing sacellum. It has an irregular plan, with two arcosolia and two apses, one of them on the right. The wall frescoes were painted at various periods. To the left of the entrance, above the tomb of St. Nemesius, is the fifth century image of a *traditio clavium* (59): at the center a beardless Christ, sitting on a globe, holds out the keys to St. Peter, whose hands are veiled; on the right, St. Paul holds the scrolls of the law in similarly veil-

ed hands; to the sides are the sain[ts] Felix, Stephen and Merita. At th[e] rear of the crypt, to the left, is a larg[e] sixth-century fresco (58) showing th[e] Madonna and Child seated on [a] richly ornamented throne; to her le[ft] are Saints Felix and Adauctus, wh[o] are introducing a deceased woma[n] named *Turtura* — a "turtle-dove" as the inscription below says, both i[n] name and in deed.

58 *Catacomb of Commodilla. Madonna enthroned with Child and with Saints Felix and Adauctus.*

59 *Catacomb of Commodilla. Delivery of the keys. Originally this scene represented the power to remit sins by opening the gates of the kingdom of heaven to the dead, in accordance with Jesus' words in the Gospels. This is its meaning in fourth and fifth century sarcophagus illustrations. But, by the time it was depicted in the catacomb of Commodilla, this meaning had been lost, and the scene had acquired the solemn tones appropriate to a representation of the conferral of hierarchical authority over the members of the Church. Beside Christ is the apostle Paul, shown bald, with a black pointed beard, in a typical portrayal. A number of votive candles rest upon his veiled hands. The fresco decorates the tomb of a martyr, as evidenced by an inscription to that effect on a painting which comes from one of the underlying layers of pictorial work. The martyr was probably Adauctus.*

58

59

60

61

60 *Catacomb of Praetextatus.*
Winter, represented in the Crypt of
the Seasons. The fresco, dated fourth
century, decorated the ceiling vault
of the crypt of St. Januarius, located
in the Spelunca Magna, where four
overlying tiers are painted with
figures alluding to the seasons:
flowers for spring, wheat for summer,
grapes for autumn and the olive
harvest for winter.

61 *Catacomb of Praetextatus. Christ*
and the Samaritan woman, in the
cubiculum of the Scala Maggiore.
The fresco, dated beginning of the
third century, is part of the
Christological cycle decorating the
walls of the cubiculum at the foot of
the stairway. The surviving episodes
are the Healing of the woman who
had an issue of blood for twelve years,
the Resurrection of Lazarus, and
another scene which has had a variety
of interpretations.

Catacomb of Praetextatus

Situated at 11 Via Appia Pignatelli, this catacomb was named after the original owner of the land, who may have been a member of the Cecili family. It dates as far back as the second century, and originated in a pagan outdoor cemetery, not far from the villa of Herodes Atticus, tutor of the sons of Marcus Aurelius. St. Januarius was buried here, as were Saints Felicissimus and Agapitus, and the martyrs Valerian, Tiburtius, Maximus and Quirinus. The catacomb is composed of several originally separate nuclei, including the so-called *Scala maggiore* area — perhaps the oldest of all, decorated with frescoes of the life of Christ — and the *Spelunca magna*, a large gallery whose chambers have masonry entrances.

Above the catacomb there are two museums containing pagan and Christian sculptures.

atacomb of Via Latina

his catacomb was discovered accidentally in 1955, during construction work in Via Dino Compagni. ther Antonio Ferrua, S.J. directed e excavations and had the findings ublished. The present entrance is a mple trap-door in the sidewalk near 8 Via Latina. The catacomb was ot meant for the Christian community. It was built for a limited number of families — at least the four ho seem to have commissioned the intings decorating the chambers, d perhaps one or two more.

he paintings were done at different mes within a relatively brief period, aced by Father Ferrua between 320 d 350, whereas the initial construction of the catacomb is dated about 5. These dates were based on four ctors: classification of the architecnic elements; discovery of two Con-antinian monograms; the presence many pagan themes (albeit with

a Christian interpretation, also a characteristic of medieval Christian art); and the character of the epigraphs. The last two factors have led other scholars to suggest earlier dates.

There are twelve frescoed chambers in this catacomb, each conventionally designated by a letter of the alphabet. According to Father Ferrua, the paintings may be divided into four groups, with all the frescoes in a given cubiculum belonging to the same group: the first group is in cubiculum A, the second in cubicula B and C, the third in chambers D, E and F, and the fourth in the six cubicula lettered from H to O (according to the Italian alphabet, which has neither J nor K).

The wealth of new elements contained in the iconography of these paintings is extraordinary, and the scenes are often modelled on prototypes heretofore unknown. Cubiculum B contains illustrations of a large number of Old Testament episodes. In the vault of the left-hand arcosolium is a fresco (62) with Adam

62 Catacomb of Via Latina. Adam and Eve in pain, and Cain and Abel with their offerings. Cubiculum B.

and Eve, each with his hand pressed against his face in a gesture of suffering and despair; approaching them are Abel, with a lamb, and Cain, with a sheaf of wheat (Genesis 4, 3-4). The destruction of Sodom (Genesis 19, 15-26) appears in the same vault (63). Lot, in flight, is old and bearded, wearing a tunic and toga, and holding his two daughters, clothed in dalmatics, by the hand. To the right is the fire-swept city and, before it, Lot's wife, transformed into a pillar of salt. On the lunette at the back of the arcosolium (65) is another fresco showing the seventy Jews sent for by Joseph as they enter Egypt (Genesis 46, 5-27). Seven persons on three carts to the left represent the seventy; in the cart at the center is Jacob, with two sons, one on each side. An Egyptian city lies to the right and the Nile, runs below.

In the vault of the right-hand ar-

63 *Catacomb of Via Latina. Lot in flight from Sodom. Cubiculum B.*

64 *Catacomb of Via Latina. Jacob's Dream. Cubiculum B.*

cosolium of the same cubiculum (64 is Jacob's Dream (Genesis 28, 10-13) This episode, and all the others ir cubiculum B are completely new tc catacomb painting. Only the Cair and Abel episode appears in some sarcophagus decoration as well.

In the left-hand niche of cubiculum C, on the right, a fresco (66) with the Sacrifice of Isaac (Genesis 22, 1-14 shows the voice of God stopping the hand of Abraham, armed with a knife and raised against his son Below, the servant, next to the ass awaits his master's return; this is the first time that this detail appears in catacomb painting. The Resurrection of Lazarus (John 11) decorates the lunette and part of the left niche of the same cubiculum (67). A beardles Jesus, rod in hand, is surrounded by a crowd of at least eighty people Lazarus' tomb is a sort of *in anti* temple, with a long flight of stair before it. Above is Moses receiving the Law (Exodus 24, 12-18) and to the right, the pillar of fire (Exodu 13, 21-22); these two episodes also appear for the first time in thi catacomb. During the Middle Ages i was common practice to combine Olc and New Testament episodes, bu here the connection is unclear.

In the rear lunette of the right hanc arcosolium in cubiculum F is a fresco representing Balaam (68). Thi episode too is drawn from the Olc Testament (Numbers 22, 21-23) anc shows Balaam astride an ass on the left and, to the right, a bearded ange brandishing a short sword. In the center a tree stands between the twc figures. In the lunette of the ar cosolium at the back of th cubiculum (69) is another episode without its like in cemetery painting Samson Smiting the Philistine (Judges 15, 14-16). Samson can be recognized by the ass's jawbone in hi right hand; on the left are the terror stricken Philistines in flight and, ov the right, the temple where the her met his death. The New Testamen episode of Jesus and the Samaritai woman at the well (John 4, 5-8), in the lunette of the left-hand an cosolium (70) seems almost t parallel the Balaam episode facing it Jesus, youthful and beardless, i clothed in a tunic and pallium, whil the woman is wearing a shorter tuni with closed shoes and earrings.

An alleged Anatomy Lesson (71) depicted on the lunette at the back o

65 *Catacomb of Via Latina. Jacob arrives in Egypt. Cubiculum B.*

66 *Catacomb of Via Latina. The sacrifice of Isaac. Cubiculum C.*

67 *Catacomb of Via Latina. Jesus resurrects Lazarus. Cubiculum C.*

68 *Catacomb of Via Latina. Balaam stopped by the angel. Cubiculum F.*

the right-hand arcosolium of chamber I, a large hexagonal room with a sexpartite vault ceiling. In this scene, a group of people of varying ages, wearing the tunic and pallium, are seated on a cloth-covered bench with, in front of them, a completely naked man stretched out upon the ground. At the center of the group, an aged and bearded gentleman, clothed in the style of the Cynics — in only a pallium — turns towards the left, and with gesture of his right hand directs the attention of the group to the area below. A man on his left reaches out to touch the stomach of the naked man. This scene has provoked much discussion. Some see in it a resuscitation or a miraculous healing, others, God surrounded by the Angels in the act of creating man. A third group claims that it is Aristotle and his disciples, and a fourth, which includes Father Ferrua, holds that it is a scene from

69

70

69 *Catacomb of Via Latina. Samson smiting the Philistines with an ass's jawbone. Cubiculum F. There were two other biblical scenes with the story of Samson in this catacomb. The painters may have wanted to establish a biblical counterpart to Hercules, the pagan God of strength.*

70 *Catacomb of Via Latina. Jesus and the Samaritan woman at the well. Cubiculum F. This scene may also be interpreted as the appearance of the Angel of God to Hagar, the handmaiden of Abraham, at the well in the wilderness where she wandered.*

everyday life alluding to the profession of the deceased man buried in the sarcophagus below. According to the last interpretation, it is a lesson in anatomy, and the deceased is the central figure wearing only the pallium and surrounded by his colleagues and disciples.

Cubiculum N is a large square chamber with a cross-vault ceiling. At the corners, four tufa columns with ionic-style marble bases and capitals support four triangular pediments resting on three large corbels. The side walls are taken up by two deep arcosolia and the rear wall gives onto cubiculum O. Unlike the latter, which is frescoed with stories from the Old and New Testament, chamber N is dedicated entirely to the myth of Hercules. This obviously pagan theme is interpreted in a Christian sense, and the hero, occasionally shown with a halo, is seen as a savior, with the accent placed on faith in human survival. The two most important episodes appear in the lunettes at the back of the arcosolia: in the one to the left, Alcestis offers to sacrifice her life for that of the dying Admetus while, in the one to the right (74), Hercules lead

Alcestis back from Hades. Behind the hero is Cerberus, guardian of the pit, and on his right Admetus waiting, lance in hand, in a house with raised curtains. On a wall inside the right-hand arcosolium is Hercules in the garden of the Hesperides (72). In this portrait, unlike the others, the hero is shown as a beardless youth. His club is leaning up against a rock and his left shoulder is covered by a Nemean lion skin. On the left is a serpent — perhaps an allusion to original sin — winding its body round the forbidden tree, instead of the dragon of the legend. But in the legend it was in fact Atlas, not Hercules, who stole the golden apples from the garden of the Hesperides.

On the opposite wall of the same arcosolium, Hercules kills the Hydra (73). Here the hero is naked, bearded, and less youthful than in the garden of the Hesperides. The other episodes depicted on the walls of this cell are Hercules and Athena clasping hands, and Hercules killing an enemy. On the vault garlands of wheat — a veiled allusion to the rewards of eternal life — set off the ribs and form rounds inside which cupids harvest and reap the crop.

71 *Catacomb of Via Latina. Anatomy Lesson. Chamber I. This interpretation of the scene is supported by the presence in the vault of frescoes showing individuals whose dedication to a life of study is indicated by a codex or scroll in their hand or by their dress.*

72 *Catacomb of Via Latina. Hercules in the garden of the Hesperides. Cubiculum N.*

73 *Catacomb of Via Latina. Hercules killing the Hydra. Cubiculum N.*

74

74 *Catacomb of Via Latina. View of the right-hand arcosolium of Cubiculum N. Notice the elegant architecture of this chamber. In the lunette, Hercules is shown bringing the heroic Alcestis back from Hades to her husband Admetus, for whom she had sacrificed her life. The legend-ary scene, symbol of conjugal love, might also serve to instruct Christians, just as other pagan myths most certainly did — the story of Cupid and Psyche, for example, and the figure of Orpheus, the musician.*

75 Ruins of the Mausoleum of St. Helen, also called "Torpignattara" (Pot Tower) because amphorae or clay pots (pignatte) were used to lighten the dome when it was built.

75

Catacomb of Saints Marcellinus and Peter

The site of this catacomb at 641 Via Casilina — formerly Via Labicana — was once called *ad duas lauros*, which indicated not only the cemetery area, but a vast estate of the emperor's including the catacomb and bounded by Porta Maggiore, Via Labicana, Via Prenestina and Centocelle. Another name for the area was *ad. S. Helenam*, because the mausoleum of St. Helen once stood here, whose ruins (75) alone survive today. On this spot, where the *Equites singulares*, guard of the Emperor, had had their necropolis from the second century on, a Christian catacomb arose during the latter part of the third century. It provided a final resting place for the bodies of the numerous Christians martyred during Diocletian's persecution. First of all there were Saints Marcellinus and Peter, who gave the catacomb its name, then St. Tiburtius, St. Gorgonius, and the Four Crowned Saints, and finally thirty or forty unknown martyrs. In the course of the fourth century, the martyrs' crypts were enlarged and embellished, and Pope Damasus (366-84) created a special monumental setting for the crypts of Tiburtius and

Gorgonius, and for Marcellinus and Peter. There were further transformations and embellishments in the fifth century, and in the sixth as well, up to the Pontificate of Honorius I (625-38).

The monumental complex which stood above the subterranean necropolis was Constantinian, and was built by order of the emperor. It consisted of a large cemeterial basilica ending in a portico, with a narthex in front (77) connected to the mausoleum that Constantine had built for his burial. A sarcophagus had even been made, but the emperor moved to Byzantium, leaving both tomb and mausoleum empty. They were later used for St. Helen, mother of Constantine. The sarcophagus (76), in dark red Egyptian porphyry, has on all four sides high-relief decorations representing victorious Romans and Barbarian prisoners. In 1153-54 it was transferred to St. John Lateran and reused by Pope Anastasius IV, but Pope Pius VI had it removed to the Vatican in 1778, and it is displayed there today in the Pio Clementine Museum.

The basilica complex as a whole was perfectly well-known in the sixteenth

century, and in 1594 the first accurate description of the monument appeared, by Antonio Bosio. There have been several excavations between the end of the last century and present times — Henry J. Stevenson's between 1896 and 1898, Friedrich W. Deichmann's in 1940 and 1954-58, and those of the Ecole Française of Rome in 1975. These have made it possible to acquire a fairly precise idea of its original appearance.

The basilica's functions, plans and dimensions were analogous to those of other Roman cemetery buildings of the period: the *Memoria apostolorum* — now San Sebastiano (Cf. p. 17) — on the Via Appia, San Lorenzo on the Tiburtina, and Sant'Agnese on the Nomentana (Cf. p. 49). Its plan was in the form of a circus, with two side aisles making a continuous deambulatory around the central nave.

The building's dimensions were noteworthy — 65 meters in length and 23 in width. The central nave was 13 meters wide and about 13.80 meters high; its light filtered through a series of large centered arch windows, and it was separated from the side aisles (6.50 meters wide and

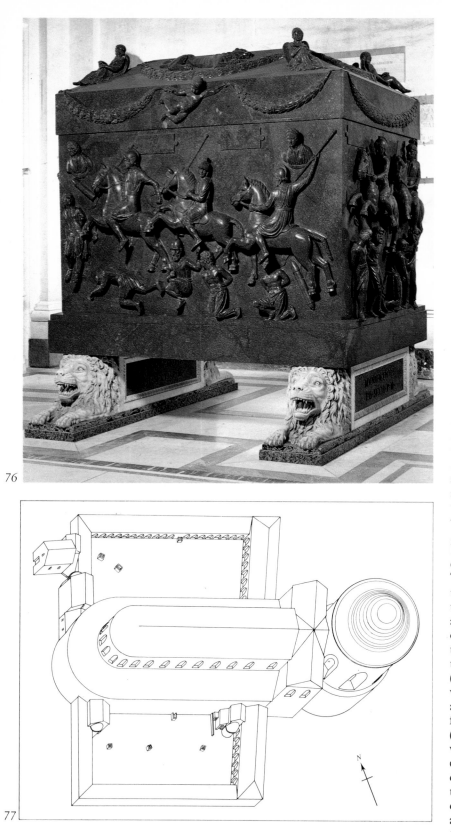

about 6.80 meters high) by a row of pillars, rectangular in section, with connecting arches. The wall painting was marbled and there was no floor — the ground was completely covered with tombs. The entrance was in the south wall of the narthex which was encompassed by the nave after the imperial mausoleum had been built to the east.

Standing before the mausoleum was an atrium, 28.40 meters long and 9.50 meters wide. It had three large openings communicating with the adjoining basilica. The mausoleum itself was over 25 meters high and had a circular plan with a diameter of 27.74 meters outside and 20.18 inside. It was illuminated by a series of large arch windows and was covered by a low, flattened dome. In the walls were seven niches, alternately semicircular and rectangular. The one on an axis with the basilica was destined for the imperial sarcophagus.

Many other mausoleums were part of the complex, some of them isolated, others backing against the south wall of the basilica, and still others either inside or backed up against the rectangular porticoes which were connected to the basilica's north and south sides at the height of the apse and narthex. But of all these, only the mausoleum of Tiburtius has survived. The basilica is dated at about 320, and the mausoleum of St. Helen between 324 and 326. The portico is earlier than either.

The catacomb frescoes, dated between the second and fourth centuries, illustrate stories from the Old and New Testaments. On the vault of one of the cubicula discovered during the excavations of 1913-15 is a mid-third-century cycle of stories of Jonah (Jonah 1, 2). At the center of the vault is the Good Shepherd and all around, alternating with praying figures, is Jonah thrown to the whale (78), Jonah at rest, and Jonah vomited out of the whale. The fourth episode of the series has been destroyed. In another cubiculum (79) the frescoed episode of Noah and the dove (Genesis 8, 11) shows the patriarch coming out of the ark in an attitude of prayer; on the left, the dove arrives with an olive branch in its beak. The chamber of Niceforus, another discovery of the excavations of 1913-15 named after its probable owner, has in the rear lunette of the arcosolium a fresco of the miracle of

76 Sarcophagus of St. Helen, kept in the Greek-cross-shaped hall in the Pio Clementine Museum in the Vatican.

77 Reconstruction of the basilica of Saints Marcellinus and Peter, with two colonnades at the sides and in front a narthex communicating with the mausoleum of St. Helen (from Guyon).

78

80

80 Catacomb of Saints Marcellinus
and Peter. Christ and the woman
who had an issue of blood for twelve
years. The lunette containing this
fresco has two other biblical scenes in-
volving women, the Samaritan
woman at the well, and the healing
of the lame woman. In the vault is a
female figure at prayer. This was un-
questionably a woman's tomb.

41

81

83

81 *Catacomb of Saints Marcellin[us]
and Peter. Daniel in the Lion's Den[.]*

82 *Catacomb of Saints Marcellin[us]
and Peter. Moses bringing forth wat[er]
from the rock.*

83 *Catacomb of Saints Marcellin[us]
and Peter. Original Sin.*

84 *Catacomb of Saints Marcellin[us]
and Peter. The Baptism of Chris[t.]
This illustration is based on th[e]
liturgical interpretation of the a[n-]
cient baptismal rite, which was a[c-]
complished by total immersion in th[e]
fountain — indicated here by th[e]
naked figure — and which include[d]
various other rites as well, such as th[e]
laying on of hands by the officia[nt]
shown in the painting. The ra[ys]
which descend from above stand f[or]
the light of the Holy Ghost, r[e-]
presented in the form of a dove. I[n]
ancient times, the sacrament of co[n-]
firmation was administered im[-]
mediately after baptism.*

85 *Catacomb of Saints Marcellin[us]
and Peter. Christ enthroned abo[ve]
the Mystical Lamb, between S[t.]
Peter and St. Paul, and hailed b[y]
the four most important marty[rs]
of the catacomb. At the center a[re]
Marcellinus and Peter, the two ma[r-]
tyrs for whom the cemetery w[as]
named. They were buried in the im[-]
mediate vicinity of this cubiculu[m.]
Tiburtius lies in the ground abov[e.]
Pilgrim guides of the seventh centu[ry]
tell us that Gorgonius dwells som[e-]
where in the subterranean area, b[ut]
his tomb has not yet been discovere[d.]*

85

he woman who had an issue of blood welve years (Mark 5, 25-35; Luke 8, 43-48) and, having touched the garment of Jesus, was healed of it (80). On the left the woman presses forward to touch the Savior's clothes, while Christ, on the right, turns about in surprise at the unexpected touch. Some date the painting midthird-century, others later, between 325 and 350.

The tomb called the "Den of Daniel" takes its name from the biblical episode (Daniel 6, 16-24) illustrated on one of its walls (81). At the center is the young and beardless prophet, his hands raised in a gesture of prayer, identified by the script above his head. Two lions at his sides, each with a paw raised, draw back before him. According to Father Ferua, who discovered it during the excavations of 1958, this fresco should be dated at the end of the third century.

In the tomb known as the "Chamber of the Four Seasons", a cycle of frescoes with four biblical stories surrounds the entrance door. They include the miracle of the loaves and the fishes, Job, Noah in the ark, and Moses bringing forth water from the rock (82). The last scene (Exodus 17, 5) is depicted beside the story of Noah and like it prefigures the Baptism. Moses, bearded and dressed in pallium and sandals, smites the rock

with the long rod in his right hand. The image of the prophet resembles that of a Greek philosopher, and probably derives from a classical prototype. Some date it during the latter half of the third century, others between 325 and 350. The chamber is not far from Niceforus's and it, too, was discovered during the excavations of 1913-15.

Another baptism illustration appears in a fresco (84) dating from the first half of the fourth century. It depicts the baptism of Christ (Matthew 3, 14-17; Mark 1, 9-11; Luke 3, 21-22; John 1, 32-33). The Redeemer is shown at the center, youthful and beardless, his feet immersed in the waters of the Jordan. Above, to the left is the dove symbolizing the Holy Ghost, with a series of rays bursting forth from its beak in a shower upon the figure of Christ. Nothing remains of the figure of the Baptist on the right but a hand, firmly placed on the head of the Savior.

On the vault of another chamber (83) is a scene depicting Original Sin

(Genesis 3, 7). Adam and Eve, naked, are shown covering themselves with two large fig-leaves, while Eve indicates the forbidden tree with the serpent, her tempter, still wound about it. Another tree on the left serves the scene as stage set. This fresco also dates from the first half of the fourth century.

In the vault of the crypt, which was once believed to contain the bodies of the martyrs of the catacomb, there is a late fourth-century painting (85), probably deriving from a contemporary apse mosaic, divided into two tiers. Above is a bearded, haloed Christ seated on a backless throne, with St. Peter and St. Paul at his side, in accordance with traditional iconography. Below, in the center, the Mystical Lamb is standing upon a hill from which the four rivers of Paradise issue. To the side are the saints, Gorgonius, Peter, Marcellinus and Tiburtius. Garlands of flowers decorate the bottom of the fresco.

43

Coemeterium Maius

This cemetery, not far from the basilica of Sant'Agnese, has its entrance at 6 Via dell'Asmara. It is called *"maius"* or *"greater"* to distinguish it from the Minor Cemetery in Via Nomentana at number 222. The name is ancient. It appears in St. Jerome's Martyrology, a compilation of testimonies on the lives of the martyrs — though, because St. Emerenziana, foster sister of St. Agnes, is buried here, the catacomb is often called by her name. The martyrs Papia, Alexander, Felix, Maurus and Victor lie here as well. The catacomb, quite long, stretches out on two levels, and has an underground basilica of sorts and numerous crypts planned for *refrigeria* or funeral banquets. These are decorated with third- and fourth-century frescoes, and provided with chairs hollowed out of the tufa, thirteen of which have been found. In addition to Old Testament episodes, the frescoes illustrate such themes as Christ giving his blessing, the faithful at prayer, and the Good Shepherd. One of the more interesting crypts was erroneously believed to be the place where St. Emerenziana was buried about the middle of the third century. It too has a chair, which in the nineteenth century was thought to have some connection with St. Peter. In the lunette of the arcosolium of an early fourth-century chapel, not far from the actual crypt of St. Emerenziana, is a painting which represents a veiled woman, richly clothed, her hands raised in a prayerful gesture (*86*); before her is a child, but only its head with two Constantinian monograms at the sides has survived. Some interpret this image as a representation of the deceased woman with her child. Others see in it the Virgin and Child, but portrayed with an iconography new to third-century catacomb painting. Ordinarily, the Madonna was shown as a full-length figure, seated, with the baby in her lap, and there were nearly always other figures around her — people at prayer and Old Testament characters. But here only the bust of Mary is shown, and she is alone with the child. At the borders of the lunette are two praying figures, one male and one female.

Although the much smaller, near-by Minor Cemetery has not even been excavated yet, the Maius has been the object of constant study and research since the nineteenth century. In fact its funeral dwellings are architecturally quite elegant, its epigraphs engraved with great precision, and its walls richly decorated with frescoes. Recently, a new martyr's tomb was discovered there, in a great staircase. But researchers have not been able to identify the inhabitant of this highly atypical underground shrine, for the Maius Cemetery martyrs are distinguished by a singular characteristic: they always appear as a liturgical group in pictures, epigraphs and documents, because in ancient celebrations in their honor, they were all commemorated together. As a result, finding out which of the martyrs is buried in any one of the frescoed or engraved tombs is a very difficult undertaking indeed. It seems that the crypt named after St. Emerenziana contains the remains of the martyrs, Victor and Alexander.

nonymous Cemetery in ia Anapo

his is one of the Via Salaria ceme-
ries, but its entrance is between
umbers 2 and 4 of Via Anapo. It was
nce held to be the cemetery of the
iordani, the most famous of the
urial sites of Via Salaria and eclipsed
nly by the Catacomb of Priscilla,
ut recent findings indicate that it
 another private cemetery. The
scovery was made accidentally, in
)21, and published by Enrico Josi.
 the cemetery are five chambers
escoed with New and Old Testa-
ent subjects. The decoration is
ated at the end of the third century.
 the first chamber, together with
aintings of Daniel in the Lion's
en, the Miracle of the Spring, Noah
 the Ark, a praying figure and the
ood Shepherd, there is an illustra-
on of the Miracle of the Loaves and
shes (Matthew 14, 13-21; Mark 6,
)-44; Luke 9, 10-17; John 6, 1-15).
sus is a youthful, beardless figure,
othed in tunic and pallium, seen
tending the long, miracle-working
d resembling Moses' rod towards
e seven baskets of bread (88).
nother fresco in the first chamber
9) shows the Resurrection of
zarus, narrated in the Gospel accord-
g to St. John (11, 1-46). Christ is on

the right, again young, short-haired
and beardless (as was usual in third
century frescoes), wearing the tunic
and pallium. He extends the selfsame
rod until it touches the grave of
Lazarus, whose body can be seen inside, bound hand and foot with
graveclothes.
In the second cubiculum are Jonah
cast forth into the sea, and Jonah
at rest; in the third, Abraham's
sacrifice, the three children in the
fiery furnace, and Christ with the
twelve apostles. In the last-named
panel (87), which decorates the ceiling vault, the young Christ is seated
in the center, surrounded by the
twelve apostles, none of whom are
distinguished by any particular sym-
bolical or character traits. All the
figures were incised in the fresh
plaster beforehand.
In the fourth and fifth cubicula the
scenes that were illustrated in the first
two chambers reappear — the praying figures, the stories of Jonah and
Noah. The other catacomb rooms
have purely ornamental decoration,
or none at all.

88

89

88 Anonymous cemetery of Via
Anapo. The Miracle of the loaves and
fishes.

89 Anonymous cemetery of Via
Anapo. The Resurrection of Lazarus.

90

90 *Catacomb of the Giordani. Praying figure, about the middle of th fourth century. This fresco is in th tomb of a woman depicted here in a attitude of prayer, with her nam GRATA written on the ochre fasce above her head. She wears a lon tunic, which has sleeves and a decora tion of "clavi" or purple bands. T the sides are a series of scenes of salva tion: the Resurrection of Lazarus t the left and, to the right, the Thre Hebrews in the Fiery Furnace an Daniel in the Lion's Den.*

91 *Catacomb of the Giordani. Riche dressed praying figure. The part c the arenarium pit where this fresco found had already become cementery by the end of the thir century, as evidenced by a medallio of Numerianus (283-284) which still in place in the lime whic seals the tomb. This painting ma have been done later, during th first part of the fourth century. Th great precision evident in the facia portrait seems to indicate that a attempt was made to reproduce rea physiognomical traits, a rare occur rence in Roman catacomb painting although it was quite frequent in th catacombs of Naples. In Rome, th praying figure usually stood for th saved soul in general, and had n connection with the deceased in dividual. In fact, prayerful femal figures decorate men's tombs, an men at prayer can be found on th tombs of women. Only on the tomb of children does the figure at praye frequently appear as a child of th same age as the deceased.*

Catacomb of the Giordani

Identified during excavations in 1966-69, this was previously believed to be the catacomb of Thraso, named thus after its owner. Its entrance is at the corner of Via Salaria and Via Taro, while the true Thraso catacomb entry lies at 1 Via Yser. In the past this cemetery — deepest of all the Roman catacombs, with its five layers of galleries — was also named Villa Massimo. It includes part of a vast *arenarium* pit in which, outside the cemetery lands, the body of Daria, a converted vestal virgin slain during the Valerian persecution (257-58), and that of her husband Crisantus lie buried — at least according to tradi- tion. A sanctuary to them built in the *arenarium* was much worshipped during the Middle Ages. Later, most of the two martyrs' relics were moved to the basilica of Santissimi Apostoli. The same *arenarium* also contained the sepulchre of a boy martyr named Maurus, and in one of its rooms wa the painting of two facing figures a prayer, one of which is here reprodu ed (*91*). Above the figures are tw stories of Jonah and Moses strikin the rock.

92

92 Catacomb of Pamphilus. Bone statue mounted in one of the catacomb loculi. It was evidently a personal object, and must have been placed on the tomb to enable the members of the dead man's family to recognize it, since it did not have the more usual and costly epigraph. Many tombs, especially the poorer ones, have signs like these for identification.

93 Catacomb of Pamphilus. View of a funeral chamber.

Catacomb of Pamphilus

Situated in the Via Paisiello section of Via Salaria Vecchia, beside the Church of St. Pamphilus, this catacomb takes its name from a martyr whose story is unknown. Other martyrs, Quirinus and Candidus were buried here as well.

It has been known of since 1594, when Antonio Bosio and Pompeo Ugonio visited some of the first level galleries. A new portion was discovered by Giovan Battista De Rossi in 1865, but the most important excavations were directed by Enrico Josi in 1920. The cemetery was composed of an area above ground and a two-storied catacomb with a mezzanine level. The tombs on the second level were found intact, and decorated with a variety of objects, such as ampullae, terracotta lamps, coins, gilded glass and statuettes (*92*). The ancient crypt consisted of a double cubiculum with an arcosolium at the back, against which stood an altar originally covered with slabs of pavonazzetto marble and porphyry. To the right of the crypt is another arcosolium with, at its extremities, two chairs hollowed out of the tufa which may have been used for the *refrigerium* rite. On the walls are graffiti with the names of some presbyters, and a marble slab containing an inscription lettered in porphyry. A niche in the adjacent gallery has a seventh-century image of the Madonna with Child, accompanied by the words DEI GENITRIX. Another funeral chamber (*93*), dating from the fourth century, has a whole series of geometric-floral frescoes and the figure of the Good Shepherd shown in a round of the vault.

ant'Agnese fuori le Mura

94 Ruins of the old Constantinian basilica of St. Agnes.

his great cemetery complex is composed of the basilica of Sant'Agnese iori le Mura (St. Agnes outside the Valls), the monumental remains of ie so-called *Coemeterium Agnetis*, id the Mausoleum of St. Constania. Under the basilica and in the surunding area lie the extended illeries of a vast catacomb, accidenlly discovered in 1865-66 and stematically excavated during the st century. The cemetery is divided ito three main networks. Two of iem are even older than the uildings of the monumental comlex, all of which are Constantinian id were erected, so it seems, on an nperial property. The first network, the left of the present basilica, is ie oldest. It is dated between the id of the second century and the eginning of the third. The second ttwork, which branches out from ihind the apse of Sant'Agnese iwards the Via Nomentana, dates ick to the third and beginning of ie fourth centuries. The third netork connects the basilica with the ausoleum of St. Constantia, and is ie most recent, dating from the urth and fifth centuries. The ibicula of this catacomb are not escoed, but numerous inscriptions, affiti and funerary objects have en found in them.

The actual basilica of Sant'Agnese is the result of a reconstruction by Pope Honorius (625-38). It stands on the side of a hill sloping down to the north west, towards the valley where Piazza Annibaliano now lies. The apse above faces onto Via Nomentana, while the façade looks down towards the valley. The edifice is partly built into the hillside, cutting into the galleries of the pre-existing catacomb. In fact, the ground floor is in direct contact with it — or rather, to be precise, with the tomb of St. Agnes, who was martyred during Decius' third-century persecution. The upper story, with galleries running above the side aisles and the narthex, has a small bridge in the area of the apse which communicates with Via Nomentana.

The basilica of Honorius' time stands on the site of a *sacellum* (or shrine) almost entirely buried in the side of the hill. This was erected simultaneously with the Constantinian basilica, as an altar over the tomb of the saint, and its level has been located at about 0.65 meters beneath the present choir. This first *ad corpus* sacellum was transformed into a small basilica during the fifth century. There are but few traces left of these two buildings, among them the remains of an apse beneath the pre-

sent apse — but it is not clear whether this belonged to the first or the second structure.

About thirty meters to the south of the *ad corpus* sacellum stood the so-called *Coemeterium Agnetis*, a large circus-shaped edifice, 98.30 meters long, 40.30 meters wide and over 17 meters high. Of this, there are only the ruins of the south perimetrical wall and of the deambulatory in which it ended to the west (94). This structure — with robust buttresses reinforcing its walls, pierced by large rectangular windows — is none other than the great cemetery basilica built by order of Constantia, daughter of Constantine, during her widow's years of residence in Rome (338-50), and dedicated by her to St. Agnes. Constantia's building had an atrium in front of it, a large central nave — 80 meters long and 17.50 wide — and 9-meter-wide side aisles linked by a continuous deambulatory in the apse area. In the choir are the remains of a hall with an apse (15 meters × 5.70), but its purpose is unknown. It is also unclear what supporting structures divided the central nave from the side aisles, whether columns, pillars or pilasters; but the building was covered with a truss roof and it certainly had no flooring, for the ground inside was entirely

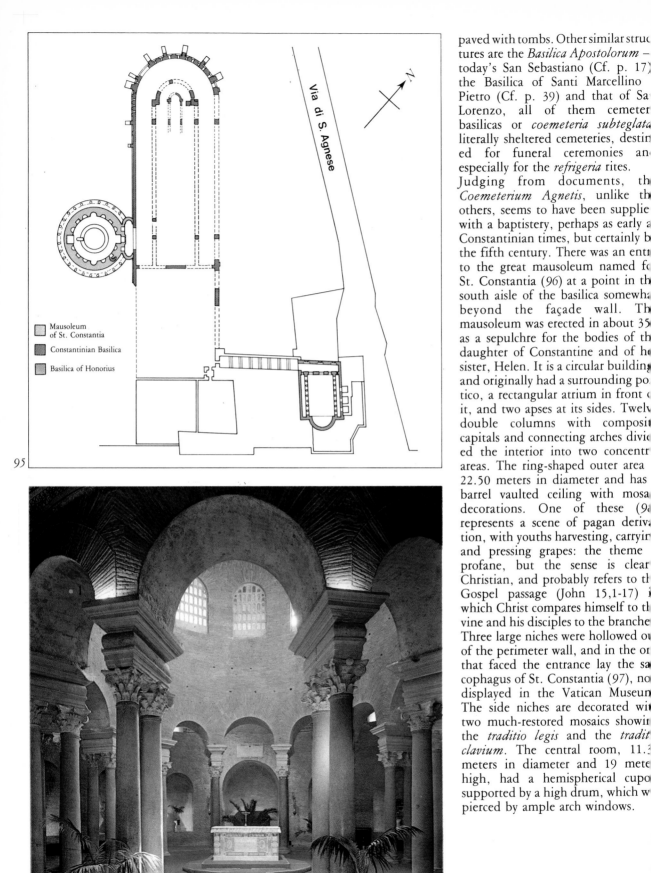

95

96

paved with tombs. Other similar structures are the *Basilica Apostolorum* –
today's San Sebastiano (Cf. p. 17)
the Basilica of Santi Marcellino
Pietro (Cf. p. 39) and that of Sa
Lorenzo, all of them cemeter
basilicas or *coemeteria subteglata*
literally sheltered cemeteries, destin
ed for funeral ceremonies an
especially for the *refrigeria* rites.
Judging from documents, th
Coemeterium Agnetis, unlike th
others, seems to have been supplie
with a baptistery, perhaps as early a
Constantinian times, but certainly b
the fifth century. There was an entr
to the great mausoleum named fc
St. Constantia (96) at a point in th
south aisle of the basilica somewha
beyond the façade wall. Th
mausoleum was erected in about 35
as a sepulchre for the bodies of th
daughter of Constantine and of hc
sister, Helen. It is a circular building
and originally had a surrounding po.
tico, a rectangular atrium in front c
it, and two apses at its sides. Twelv
double columns with composit
capitals and connecting arches divic
ed the interior into two concentr
areas. The ring-shaped outer area
22.50 meters in diameter and has
barrel vaulted ceiling with mosa
decorations. One of these (9t
represents a scene of pagan deriva
tion, with youths harvesting, carryir
and pressing grapes: the theme
profane, but the sense is clear
Christian, and probably refers to th
Gospel passage (John 15,1-17) i
which Christ compares himself to th
vine and his disciples to the branche
Three large niches were hollowed ou
of the perimeter wall, and in the on
that faced the entrance lay the sa
cophagus of St. Constantia (97), no
displayed in the Vatican Museun
The side niches are decorated wit
two much-restored mosaics showir
the *traditio legis* and the *tradit
clavium*. The central room, 11.3
meters in diameter and 19 mete
high, had a hemispherical cupo
supported by a high drum, which w
pierced by ample arch windows.

95 Plan of the complex of monuments of St. Agnes. The basilica of Honorius, the Mausoleum of St. Constantia, and the still-existent structures of the Constantinian basilica are all indicated. The rectory of Pius IX, and the stairway leading down from it to the level of Honorius' basilica, are shown in black. Visible at the center of the large circus-shaped basilica — a typical Constantinian structure — is the small sanctuary discovered during excavations in 1954. Shrines of this sort are not ordinarily found in circus-shaped basilicas — the basilica of Saint Marcellinus and Peter, the basilica of San Lorenzo, etc. — unless they are devotional tombs or areas reserved for funeral banquets (from Perrotti).

96 Mausoleum of St. Constantia. View of the interior.

97 Sarcophagus of St. Constantia, in the Pio-Clementine Museum in the Vatican.

98 Mausoleum of St. Constantia. Mosaic with the grape harvest.

97

98

51

San Paolo fuori le Mura

99 Interior of the basilica of San Paolo fuori le mura.

The basilica of San Paolo fuori le Mura (St. Paul's outside the Walls) stands on Via Ostiense, two kilometers from the Aurelian Walls and the Porta San Paolo. The present edifice is a reconstruction (1825-54) of the building destroyed in the fire of 1823. It has maintained the design, the dimensions and, in part, the surviving structures of the older church. The quadriporticus on its west front was built *ex novo* between 1890 and 1928.

In pre-Theodosian times, perhaps under Constantine, there was another small basilica on this site, built over a first or second century monument, which was the tomb and commemorative monument of the apostle Paul. The ruins of the apse, brought to light during the excavations of 1850, show that its orientation was the reverse of that of the present church. In 384, or perhaps 386, on the same site, the three reigning emperors, Theodosius I, Valentinian II and Arcadius began the construction of a new, large basilica, which

was finished under Honorius in 402-03. The new basilica was created to give the tomb of St. Paul a monumental setting, as had been done in Constantinian times with the basilica of S. Peter which was, in many ways, its prototype. In front of the edifice on Via Ostiense was a large porticoed courtyard. Inside, five aisles separated by columns with connecting arches led to the transept, which was continuous, as in St. Peter's, and slightly projecting beyond the outer walls of the side aisles. The apse to its east was stately, wide as the central nave. The funeral monument to St. Paul was not located on the chord of the apse, as was its twin in St. Peter's, but on a spot quite close to the central nave. The column shafts were plundered from other buildings, but the capitals were specially prepared, composite in the central nave, Corinthian in the side aisles. The dimensions of the basilica were magnificent, surpassing those of all the other basilicas of its time. The breadth of the central nave

was 24.22 meters, its length 89.87 meters and its height 30.77 meters. The inner side aisles were 8.96 meters wide and 16.22 meters high, the outer ones, 8.88 meters and 11.65 meters. The depth of the transept was 24.20 meters, its width 71.01, and its height 26.81. The atrium was 66.80 meters wide and 59.08 meters long. Twenty-one windows flooded light upon the central nave, and the transept was illuminated by twelve arch windows and twelve round ones — but the apse and side aisles had no outside openings.

Not much is known of the original mosaic decoration of the basilica which was completely redecorated with stucco and frescoes under Leo I (440-61). More important work was done under Gregory I (590-604), who raised the transept level by 90 centimeters and created a new setting for the tomb of St. Paul, building above it, among other things, the principal altar of the basilica. The addition of a baptistery is attributable to Pope Symmachus.

Santa Maria Maggiore

100 *Interior of the basilica of Santa Maria Maggiore.*

Towering above the summit of the Esquiline hill is the basilica of Santa Maria Maggiore, dedicated from the first to the "*theotokos*". Its façade is set on the peak of the hill facing south east, and its naves extend north west along an artificial terrace. A series of excavations — some old, some recent — have located the remains of several pre-existing Roman structures below the present building. In the past a connection was thought to exist between Santa Maria Maggiore and the basilica built — according to the *Liber Pontificalis* — by Pope Liberius (352-66) *iuxta macellum Liviae*. But according to recent studies, there is no link whatsoever between the two buildings. The construction of Santa Maria Maggiore is placed between 400 and 430, and its completion shortly before or during the Pontificate of Sixtus III (432-40), who is credited with having gathered the church.

The appearance of the building today is partly the result of restructuring by the architect Ferdinando Fuga be-

tween 1741 and 1747, and partly of modifications in the apse area carried out during the Romanesque period. Nevertheless, the aisles still look very much as they originally did. The fifth-century basilica, like the present one, had three naves, the central one ending in an apse. According to the *Liber Pontificalis* there was a quadriporticus in front, but no traces of this structure have been found. The total width of the building including the perimeter walls was about 35 meters. The central nave, excluding the apse, was 71.56 meters in length, between 17.45 meters and 17.60 meters in width, and 18.35 meters in height at the point where the ceiling began. Then as now it was separated from the aisles by twenty columns on each side. These had bases of varying heights, and were crowned by Ionic capitals and connected by a classical architrave. Bordering the arch windows above the architrave were pilaster strips with Corinthian capitals, placed in line with the columns below. Beneath the

windows, stucco niches framed mosaic panels illustrating Old Testament stories. The apse was originally connected to the triumphal arch and lighted by five large arch windows. All the mosaics in the central nave were done when the church was built, although there was a brief lapse of time between the making of those on the side walls and that of their slightly later fellows on the triumphal arch. Stories from Genesis are illustrated on the left wall, stories from Exodus, Numbers and Joshua on the right. Among the latter (*101*) is a scene believed to represent Moses as a young boy adopted by the Pharaoh's daughter (Exodus 11, 4-10). The princess is seated on a small throne with a tympanum, on the left. The maiden pushing the child has been identified as Moses' sister, and the woman holding the basket of fruit on the far right as his mother. In the lower part of the same panel, Moses is shown in discussion with the wise men of Egypt. Another scene illustrated on the right wall of the cen-

53

101

102

101 Santa Maria Maggiore. Mosaic with Moses handed over to the Pharaoh's daughter.

102 Santa Maria Maggiore. The crossing of the Jordan.

tral nave (*102*) shows Joshua leading the Jews across the Jordan (Joshua 3, 15-17). Below, the same panel depicts the Jewish warrior sending two spies to Jericho (Joshua 2, 1). The mosaics of the triumphal arch celebrate the Council of Ephesus (*431*), which proclaimed the dogma of Mary's divine motherhood. The mosaic artists, with wonderful skill, sought to express this sublime attribute. The Virgin is always accompanied by a retinue of Angels in the evangelical scenes illustrated. All of the episodes regard the infancy of Jesus: after the Annunciation comes the Adoration of the Magi, the Presentation in the Temple, the Flight into Egypt, and the Slaughter of the Innocents. The cities of Jerusalem and Bethlehem are shown below. At the center of the arch is the Pope's dedicatory inscription, "Built by Sixtus the Bishop for the people of God". The Pope was Sixtus III.

Santa Sabina

The basilica of Santa Sabina, standing at the top of the Aventine hill with one flank facing the Tiber valley, has a south-west/north-east orientation and was built on a series of pre-existing structures, some of them partially encompassed by the new edifice. One of these old structures is the façade of an *insula* type Roman house with a shop on the ground floor, which was incorporated in the perimeter wall of the basilica's south nave. Another, part of a building sometimes identified as the *titulus* of Santa Sabina and extending in the same north-easterly direction as today's church, was used to make up the outer wall of the narthex, to the southwest.

The basilica was restored to its early Christian appearance during the present century. It was built during the Pontificate of Celestine I (422-32) by a Dalmatian priest, Peter of Illyria, and finished during that of Sixtus III (432-40). The plan is quite simple, with a central nave ending in an apse, and two side aisles. In front of the façade is the narthex that once had two side entrances from the parallel streets flanking the basilica: to the west was the *Vicus Altus* entry, now gone, and to the east that of *Vicus Armilustri*, today Via S. Sabina. Leading to the interior of the church were three doors instead of the

present-day two. Altogether, the basilica with the narthex is 62.98 meters long and 24.80 meters wide. Two rows of twenty-four Corinthian columns with connecting arches separate the side aisles from the central nave, which is lighted by a series of ample arch windows set in line with the intercolumn. Three great openings, also with centered arches, illuminate the apse, while the windows in the side aisles are smaller.

Much of the interior decoration of the fifth century basilica has been lost. An *opus sectile* frieze — the incrustation is of marble — survives in the central nave above the colonnade, and shows a masonry curtain surmounted by a fascia with rounds, squares and rectangles. Aligned with each column is a military insignia, symbol of the triumph of Christ and His faith throughout the Empire. Not a trace remains of the decoration above, but it too may have been in *opus sectile*, a type of inlay in which the pieces are cut into shapes that follow the lines of the pattern or picture. Also in the central nave is a large mosaic fascia inscribed with the church dedication. The Latin text reads: "When Celestine had the supreme apostolic dignity/and shone through all the world as the first of Bishops/This marvel was created by a priest of Rome, a native of Il-

lyria/Peter, a man worthy of this name for his nourishment from birth was in the wake of Christ/Rich for the poor, poor for himself/Having shunned the good things of the present life/He well deserves to hope for the gift of the future life". To the sides are two female figures, representing the Church's origins in east and west: on the left, the Synagogue with the book of the Old Testament; on the right, the Church with that of the New. Originally St. Peter and St. Paul and the symbols of the four evangelists were shown above.

The wooden door at the entrance to the central nave was probably built at the same time as the basilica. Made of either cedar or cypress, it is decorated on both sides. The front ornamentation consists of a series of eighteen rectangular panels — there were originally twenty-eight — of which the larger ones are set vertically and the smaller ones horizontally. The whole is framed by a frieze of twisted vine branches with zoological motifs. The panels depict stories of Moses, Elijah and Christ. The entire group is held to be an illustration of St. Augustine's famous comparison of the Law, the Prophets and the Gospels. The iconography suggests oriental, perhaps Syrian, influences and derives from two different kinds of illuminated manuscript. The

104

105

104 *Interior of the basilica of Santa Sabina.*

105 *Santa Sabina. Wooden door: the Crucifixion.*

106 *Santa Sabina. Wooden door: three of Christ's miracles.*

106

source of the large panel compositions is the *rotulus* or illustrated roll miniature, that of the small panel decoration is the *codex* or bound book miniature. The panel with the crucifixion (*105*) is the oldest sculptural representation of this theme: triumphant over death, bearded, wide-eyed and halo-less Christ stands between the two robbers; there is a mere hint of the presence of the crosses, and the figures are naked, except for the *subligaculum* round their loins. In the background are three stylized buildings. Another panel illustrates three of Christ's miracles, all taken from the Gospel according to St John (*106*). The marriage of Cana (2, 1-11) is below; in the center is the miracle of the loaves and fishes (6, 1-15); and above, the healing of the man who was blind from birth (9, 1-33). On the back of the door is a series of floral motifs inspired by the botanical treatise of Dioscorides, an Alexandrian physician of the first century. In 1836 the door was restored.

56

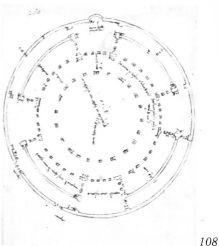

107 *Aerial view of the church of San-to Stefano Rotondo.*

108 Cronaca, *plan of Santo Stefano Rotondo (Florence, Gabinetto dei Disegni e delle Stampe degli Uffizi).*

Santo Stefano Rotondo

The church of Santo Stefano Rotondo, rising on the slopes of the Celio with its entrance on Via del Celio, has at various times in the course of the past centuries been taken for a temple, a *macellum* — or ancient market —, and a basilica. It was built by Pope Simplicius between 468 and 483, and decorated with mosaics and marble incrustations by Popes John I and Felix IV between 523 and 530. Unfortunately the decoration is lost to us today. Santo Stefano Rotondo had no resident clergy, and probably depended for them on St. John Lateran. Although no relic has ever been found nor the presence of one documented, the martyr worshipped here was surely St. Stephen — to whom, after all, the church was dedicated.

The original structure can still be recognized in the present edifice despite the ravages of time and the modifications and restorations of past centuries. The plan (*108*) consists of three concentric circular areas enclosed by a perimeter wall whose diameter is 65.80 meters. The external area, 10.60 meters wide, suffered the greatest damage. Originally it was divided symmetrically into eight sections, four located at each of the cardinal points and four at the diagonal to them. There were eight entrances into the diagonal sections, and they led into curvilinear covered passageways, parallel to the outer wall and communicating with the four radial chapels which occupied the cardinal sections. In each of the diagonal sections, free space, towards the interior of the edifice, was created by the curvilinear entrance passageways, and in these spaces — perhaps once open-air courtyards — there were elegant Serlian three-mullioned opening communicating with the radial chapels. The roof over the chapels was higher than that over the diagonal sections, giving the building a cruciform appearance. An arcaded colonnade, now obstructed, separated the outer area from the middle one and created a 9.40 meter-wide circular nave, communicating with the radial chapels, and receiving light from the courtyards in the diagonal sections. A second circular colonnade of twenty-two Ionic columns with beams above separated the nave in the middle area from the rotunda in the center. The rotunda diameter was 22.50 and its height about the same. Its light came from twenty-two arch windows in the tambour, which supports the roof just under the ceiling of the nave. These windows — partly obstructed today — were aligned with the intercolumns below. There are no traces of an altar in the rotunda center, and it is possible that it was always in the east chapel, as it is now.

Santa Pudenziana

109 Basilica of Santa Pudenziana. Apse mosaic with Christ the Teacher among the Apostles.

The basilica of Santa Pudenziana, located in the valley separating the Esquiline from the Viminal hill, has its façade fronting on Via Urbana, the former *Vicus Patricius*, and its apse on Via Balbo; but its appearance, transformed by century after century of restoration, is no longer that of the basilica built in early Christian times — which was itself the result of the renovation, begun in about 387-90 and completed in about 398, of two pre-existent Roman buildings, a mid-second-century house and a thermal basilica. It is the only example in Rome of a civil basilica put to religious purposes. The house may have been the old *titulus* of Pudens. If so, it would explain why the writing on the book held by the Savior in the apse mosaic refers not to the hypothetical St. Pudenziana or Potentiana, but to an equally hypothetical Roman senator named Pudens, friend to the apostles, who made his home into a church. The same apse mosaic had another inscription, lost to us today. It gave the donors' names — Ilicius, Maximus and Leopardus — and made it possible to date the comple-

tion of decorative work on the church, of which the mosaic is the only surviving part, to the period of Pope Innocent I (401-17).

The mosaic (*109*) shows Christ enthroned in majesty with the apostles, who form a semicircle around Him. He is clothed in purple and holds in his left hand the book inscribed DOMINUS CONSERVATOR ECCLESIAE PUDENTIANAE, while His right is raised in an oratorical gesture. The Savior is represented according to a scheme clearly deriving from the Imperial iconography of Christ the King, which is associated with a theme very common in the fifth century, that of Christ Teaching. To either side of Him are Peter and Paul. Behind them two female figures symbolizing the *ecclesia ex circumcisione* and the *ecclesia ex gentibus* are shown placing crowns on their heads. At the Savior's feet the Mystical Lamb stretches its head towards the dove, symbol of the Holy Ghost. In the background, a curved portico with some buildings rising behind it — among them a rotunda and an octagonal edifice — may very well represent holy places in

Palestine. The portico might correspond to the Anastatian church in Jerusalem, and the monuments behind it to the basilica on Golgotha, to the Imbomon on the Mount of Olives, or to the Church of the Nativity in Bethlehem. A great jewelled cross rises on a mound behind the Redeemer. At its sides, in heaven, are the symbols of the four evangelists — eagle, ox, lion and angel. The mosaic has suffered repeated damage, the worst of it during restoration of the church in 1588. Two apostles and the Mystical Lamb are missing. It has also been restored many times over, in the sixteenth and seventeenth centuries in fresco, in the nineteenth in mosaic, and as a result almost the entire right-hand side has been redone: in fact, all that remains of the original is the overall composition scheme and the head of St Peter.

anti Cosma e Damiano

he basilica of Santi Cosma e Da-
iano stands at the edge of the
oman Forum, beside the basilica of
axentius, with its present-day en-
ance facing on Via dei Fori Im-
eriali — the original one was on Via
acra. Since pre-existing Constanti-
an civil structures were used to con-
ruct the basilica, it cannot initially
ave been a cult edifice. The rotun-
a, serving as entrance to the great
ll and apse, is Constantinian as
ell. The transformation of the
uilding from civil to religious use
ok place under Pope Felix IV
26-30), who simply decorated the
ose with a mosaic, which is still in its
ace today. It represents Christ (*110*)
oised upon a ladder of clouds, in
olden robes, with the scroll of the
aw in His hands. Below, on the
anks of the Jordan, the river of
demption, and surrounded by
enery not terrestrial, but rather sug-
esting Paradise, St. Peter and St.
aul present to the Savior the two
tular saints of the church, St.
osmas and St. Damian, in whose
eiled hands are the crowns which
mbolize their martyrdom. The
ene is completed by the background figures of the donor, Felix
IV, and St. Theodore, both identified in script, and two palms symbolizing resurrection. In the fascia
below, the Mystical Lamb, symbol of
Christ, is shown beside twelve sheep,
representing the twelve apostles. The
general theme of the mosaic is the
Maiestas Domini. Its representation,
linked to the apocalyptic theme of
Christ the Judge appearing on Judg-
ment Day, was to become very
popular during the Middle Ages,
albeit with a different iconography.
In this typically Roman form, typical
also of Latium, the reference is to the
following Gospel text (Matthew 24,
30) "And then... they shall see the
Son of man coming in the clouds of
heaven with power and great glory".
Over the centuries the mosaic has suffered great damage, and repeated
restoration, especially during the sixteenth and seventeenth centuries.
The renewed portions include the entire left-hand area with Felix IV and
the lower part of the figure of St.
Cosmas beside it, as well as part of
the figure of Christ, and the upper
area of the half dome with the hand
of the Eternal Father. Felix IV is a
seventeenth century reconstruction
— and probably a faithful one — of
the image destroyed in the sixteenth
century when Gregory XIII had it
painted over with the figure of St.
Gregory the Great.

The mosaic on the triumphal arch
was completed later, during the Pontificate of Sergius I, between 692 and
701. Here too the theme represented
is the apocalypse, but the reference is
directly to the Revelation of St. John
the Divine (4,5). At the center, inside a *clipeus* or shield, is the jewelled
throne, and upon it sits the Mystical
Lamb with the cross. The seven seals
lie on the footrest still intact. To the
side are the seven jewelled lamps of
fire, four angels, and the symbols of
the evangelists; below, the twenty-
four elders dressed in white raiment
raise the crowns on their veiled
hands.

111 Pio Christian Museum. Grave stone of Seberus.

112 Pio Christian Museum. Sarcophagus of the Three Shepherds.

113 Pio Christian Museum. Oval or tub-shaped sarcophagus.

114 Pio Christian Museum. "Dogmatic" sarcophagus.

Pio Christian Museum

The museum is housed in a new building in the Vatican, erected after 1963 by the Passarelli brothers to contain the collections until then on display in the Lateran Palace, which Pope John XXIII had decided to reappoint the seat of the Vicariate. The collection is essentially that created by Pius IX in 1854, when he entrusted Father Giuseppe Marchi with organization of the sculptures and Giovan Battista De Rossi with that of the inscriptions, though the new arrangement is the work of Enrico Josi, assisted by Father Umberto Fasola. The gallery of Christian sarcophagi, the richest and most important collection of its kind, makes it possible to follow the chronological, iconographical and stylistic evolution of Early Christian sculpture for at least 150 years, until the new custom of burying the dead beneath the floors of cemetery basilicas came to be adopted in Rome.

The sarcophagus represented the most luxurious form of burial. It was a rectangular or oval shaped casket covered by a lid, either pitched in two directions like a roof or flat, with a tablet for inscriptions in the center, and with scenes sculpted on lid and sides drawn mainly from the Old and New Testaments. The favored episodes from the latter were miracles showing the Savior's omnipotence — resurrections, healings, and the miracle of the loaves and fishes. Father Marchi put together the Lateran collection by reconstructing the mutilated and truncated sarcophagi in the Christian Museum of the Vatican Library, and by having others transferred from Roman churches, basilicas and catacombs to the new site. In the present display, the sarcophagi still have their old inventory numbers, which are listed in the Museum catalogue published by J. Ficker in 1894 and in F.W. Deichmann's *Repertorium* of 1967. One inscription, on a gravestone (111) of the first half of the fourth century, has a graffito with the name of the owner, Seberus, and a cask on the left representing his trade. In the center, enclosed in a stylized laurel wreath, the monogram of Constantine appears, with the letters of the Apocalypse ω and A, the end and the beginning, to the side. A particularly interesting sarcophagus (112) with decoration on four sides has, on the front, three shepherds standing on ornamented pedestals, the bearded central figure carrying a ram on his shoulder, the beardless youths on either side of him each with a ewe. They are dressed in short tunics with gaiters and boots, and carry the shepherds crook and knapsack. The surface between these figures is crowded with the representation of a wine harvest, at which winged genii clamber up the vine branches to pick the grapes and place them in a vat for pressing, shown at the bottom right. At the top, Psyche rushes off towards a resting genie, with a basketful of grapes in her hands; another genie is milking a goat at the bottom left. The decoration of the sides of this sarcophagus, in two tiers, symbolizes the four seasons by illustrating the work that typifies each of them. The back has a transenna-like decoration with scale motifs. The sarcophagus was found in the Vigna Buonfiglioli near the cemetery of Praetextatus, to the left of the Appian Way, and dates from the latter part of the fourth century. Another oval tub-shaped sarcophagus (113) has a sculpture with two crouching rams to the sides and the Good Shepherd in the center between two trees, with a ram on his shoulder and two more at his feet. He is shown turning towards a veiled woman in an attitude of prayer. A second woman beside her is seated, with a scroll in her left hand, and her right hand raised as she converses. On the left, two men in philosophers' dress are engaged in a discussion; the one in the center is seated, and holds in his hands a partly opened scroll. A sun dial can be seen behind. The two seated figures are held to be the couple who commissioned the sarcophagus, which was found in 1888 in Via Salaria, near the mausoleum of Licinius Peto, and purchased by Leo XIII in 1891. Most scholars place it in the period of Gallienus (253-60).

The "dogmatic" sarcophagus (114) is so-called because the reliefs on the front, the only side with decoration, are of profoundly religious inspiration. They are arranged in two tiers. Above, from right to left, are: the creation of man and woman by the Holy Trinity; the Savior giving Adam and Eve means of sustenance after the sin; a *Clipeus* with busts of both the deceased (only sketched in); the Miracle of Cana; the Miracle of the loaves and fishes; and the Resurrection of Lazarus. Below, from left to right: the Epiphany; the Healing of the man who was blind from birth; Daniel in the Lion's Den; Christ prophesying to Peter that he should deny Him thrice; and the Capture of St. Paul and St. Peter. The sarcophagus was found in 1838 during work on the foundation of the baldachin of San Paolo fuori le Mura, and is dated latter half of the fourth century. The Epiphany also appears on the right side of the lid of a now fragmentary sarcophagus (115). On the casket were the Entrance into Jerusalem, the Delivery of the Law, and Christ before Pilate. The sarcophagus, from the latter part of the fourth century,

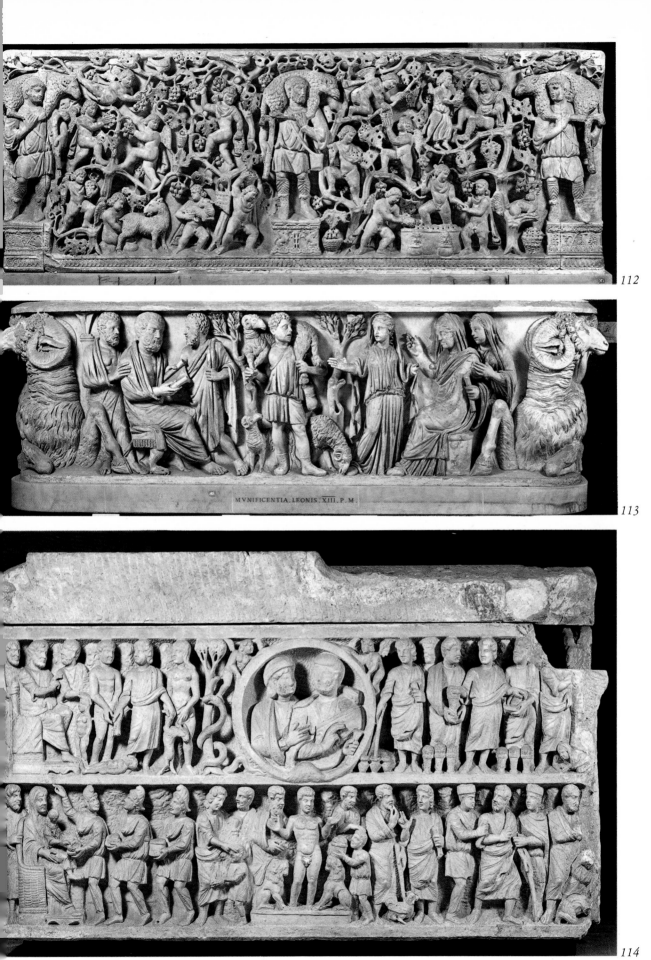

112

113

MVNIFICENTIA · LEONIS · XIII · P · M ·

114

115

116

117

115 *Pio Christian Museum. Fragment of sarcophagus lid with Adoration of the Magi.*

116 *Pio Christian Museum. The gravestone of Alexandra.*

117 *Pio Christian Museum. Sarcophagus with Christ and the Apostles.*

118 *Pio Christian Museum. The Good Shepherd.*

119 *Pio Christian Museum. The Good Shepherd.*

comes from the Vatican necropoli. On a gravestone, also from the fourth century, (*116*), the deceased is portrayed at the center with her arms raised in a gesture of prayer, while a dove presents her with a crown. The inscription ALEXANDRA IN PACE appears at the side. A last sarcophagus (*117*) represents a youthful Christ dressed as a shepherd with the

twelve apostles surrounding him. Twelve sheep lie at their feet. As background to the scene, two young shepherds are shown moving among flocks of sheep and trees. This sarcophagus, of the second half of the fourth century, comes from San Lorenzo fuori le Mura.

Completing the collection are a series of casts of particularly important pieces not belonging to the museum, a mosaic portrait of a deceased couple coming from Agro Verano and donated by Benedict XV, and a bell from Canino in the province of Viterbo, dating from the eighth century and held to be the oldest example of this instrument. There are also two statuettes of the Good Shepherd, both accurately following the description in the Gospel passage (Luke 15, 4,5). They portray a curly-haired youth, dressed in a short tunic belted at the waist, with a lamb on his shoulder. In the older statuette (*119*), dating from the first half of the fourth century, the shepherd has a knapsack slung over his back; the

lower part of the tunic and the le[...] have been restored. The piece w[...] part of the Mariotti collection in t[...] Lateran Museum since the eighteen[...] century. In the second statue (*118*) from the second half of the four[...] century, the shepherd holds a gnarl[...] and knotty stick in his hand. The i[...] age of the devotee bringing offerin[...] to the temple also occurs in paga[...] sculpture, in forms similar to th[...] But these statuettes have a differe[...] meaning, and the image clearly refe[...] to Christ, at once shepherd and Lam[...] (John 10, 11-18).

The epigraphical collection create[...] by De Rossi is on display in a sectio[...] closed to the public and dedicated e[...] clusively to scholars. Here, inscrip[...] tions of various origin are united [...] an organic grouping. The collectio[...] includes the inscriptions accum[...] lated in the storage rooms of th[...] Museum and the Vatican Libra[...] after the Pontificate of Pius VII, tho[...] coming from the excavations at Ost[...] and from research explorations of th[...] catacombs, those from Agro Verano[...]

onated by the municipality of
ome, and those found by De Rossi
various monasteries, churches and
hapels. At a later date the collection
as enriched by a group of Hebrew
scriptions. De Rossi divided the
aterial into two groups, classifying
he *Inscriptiones sacrae* — a precious
urce of primary material for the
storian of Christianity and its cult
onuments during the first centuries
-, and the other *Inscriptiones selec-*
e — a selection of monuments ac-
rding to their importance. The first
oup was divided into inscriptions
garding sacred buildings, their
venues and their donations, and in-
riptions in praise of the martyrs.
he latter was again subdivided into
ree groups; the first one chrono-
gical, containing inscriptions whose
ates were certain, until the year 365;
e second dogmatic, including
pigraphs with formulas which ex-
ound and illustrate faith, discipline,
clesiastical hierarchy, civil condi-
ons, and family; and the third
pographical, dividing the material
cording to the Christian cemeteries
f Rome from which it came. De
ossi's classification has been
spected, as far as possible, in the
resent arrangement of the material.

119

GLOSSARY

AEDICULA. Small building often in the shape of a classical temple, covering a statue or a picture.

ARCOSOLIUM. Sepulchral monument made out of an arch or a sarcophagus, fitted into a niche that generally has a semicircular vault.

BASILICA. Edifice on a longitudinal axis, consisting of a central nave separated from two or four lateral naves by rows of columns. It is endowed with an apse and often an atrium or narthex. Employing a structure originally used by the Romans for civil purposes, the early Christians adopted the basilica plan for the centers of their cult.

CUBICULUM. The bedroom in a Roman house where the children and the servants slept. In the catacombs, it was the crypt or chapel, which opened from the sides of the galleries and contained one or more arcosolia.

DALMATIC. Vestment based on the tunic design, with long sleeves and two strips of red material ornamenting it. It was worn by the Romans until the second century A.D., and thereafter by Christian clergy for liturgical celebrations.

HYPOGEUM. Private underground sepulchre in which one or more deceased persons were entombed. This name was also given to several catacombs.

LOCULI. Long, horizontal cavities hollowed out of the catacomb walls, one atop the other, which held corpses.

MARTYRY. Church constructed over the tomb of a martyr. It can be distinguished from the basilica because it always has a central plan.

MEMORIAL. Sepulchral monument built over the tomb of a martyr or a saint.

NARTHEX. Transverse vestibule preceding the façade of the basilica and consisting of a colonnade or a quadriporticus. Unbaptized Christians were permitted to enter into the narthex.

PALLIUM. Part of the liturgical dress reserved for Papal use, the pallium is a narrow band of white material that hangs down over the wearer's chest.

SACELLUM. Small sepulchre or chapel built over the tomb of a saint or martyr.

TROPHY. Monument over the tomb of a martyr, or on the spot where a martyrdom took place. The name derives from the notion common among the early Christians that a martyrdom was a victory of faith.

120 *Catacomb of Pamphilus. Rear lunette of an arcosolium with a pair of doves and garlands of flowers.*

BIBLIOGRAPHY

J. WILPERT, *Le pitture delle catacombe romane*, Roma 1903.
R. KRAUTHEIMER, W. FRANKL, S. CORBETT, A. FRAZER, *Corpus basilicarum Cristianorum Romae*, I-V, Città del Vaticano 1937-1977.
F. W. DEICHMANN, A. TSCHIRA, *Das Mausoleum der Kaiserin Helena und die Basilika der heiligen Marcellinus und Petrus an der via Labicana von Rom* - «Jahrbuch des deutschen archäologischen Instituts» LXXII, 1957.

A. FERRUA, *Le pitture della nuova catacomba della via Latina*, Città del Vaticano 1960.
A. P. FRUTAZ, *Il complesso monumentale di S. Agnese,* Città del Vaticano 1960.
U. FASOLA, *La basilica dei SS. Nereo e Achilleo e la catacomba di Domitilla,* Roma 1965.
F. W. DEICHMANN, *Repertorium der christlich-antiken Sarkophage*, I, Wiesbaden 1967.
A. NESTORI, *Repertorio topografico delle pitture delle catacombe romane*, Roma 1975.
U. FASOLA, *Pietro e Paolo a Roma. Orme sulla roccia,* Roma 1980.